▰▰▰ *The Magical Classroom*

INSTRUCTIONAL
IMc MEDIA CENTER
C.W. POST CAMPUS OF L.I.U.

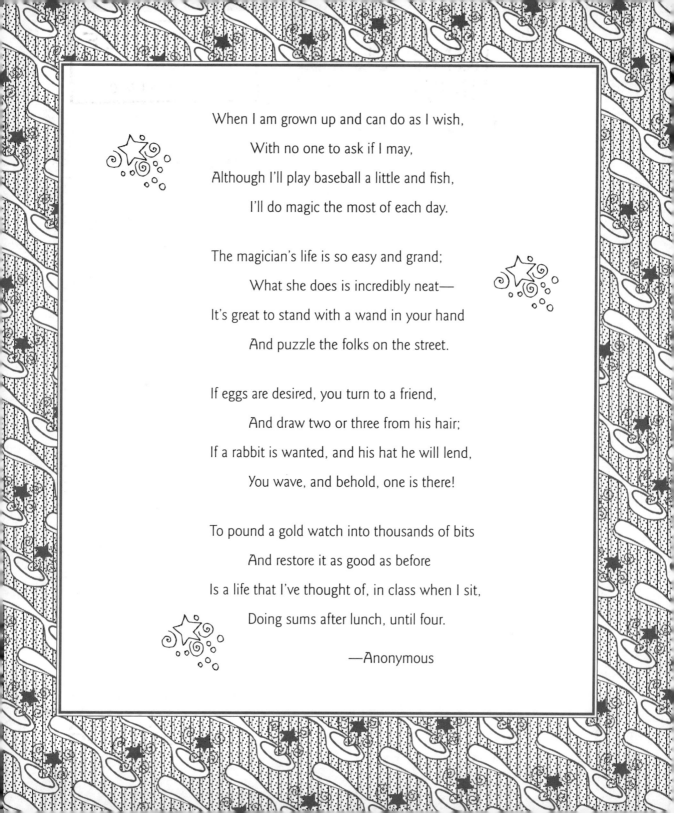

When I am grown up and can do as I wish,
With no one to ask if I may,
Although I'll play baseball a little and fish,
I'll do magic the most of each day.

The magician's life is so easy and grand;
What she does is incredibly neat—
It's great to stand with a wand in your hand
And puzzle the folks on the street.

If eggs are desired, you turn to a friend,
And draw two or three from his hair;
If a rabbit is wanted, and his hat he will lend,
You wave, and behold, one is there!

To pound a gold watch into thousands of bits
And restore it as good as before
Is a life that I've thought of, in class when I sit,
Doing sums after lunch, until four.

—Anonymous

The Magical Classroom

Exploring Science, Language, and
Perception with Children

Michael J. Strauss

bee line
BOOKS

Heinemann
Portsmouth, NH

.ne Books

ın imprint of Heinemann
A division of Reed Elsevier Inc.
361 Hanover Street
Portsmouth, NH 03801-3912
Offices and agents throughout the world

We are grateful to the following publisher for granting permission to reprint material from a previously published work:
Excerpts from *Your Most Enchanted Listener* by Wendell Johnson. Copyright © 1956 by Harper & Brothers, renewed © 1984 by Edna Johnson. Reprinted by permission of HarperCollins Publishers, Inc.

All the effects and illusions described in this book, as well as the described materials, are intended for use by children age eight and above. For younger children, the materials and procedures may be hazardous.

Acquisitions: Leigh Peake
Production and copyediting: Renée M. Nicholls
Cover and interior design: Greta D. Sibley
Cover art: Lynn Jeffery
Decorative embellishments: Stephanie Peterson and Greta D. Sibley
Manufacturing: Louise Richardson

Library of Congress Cataloguing-in-Publication Data
Strauss, Michael J.
     The magical classroom : exploring science, language, and
perception with children / Michael J. Strauss.
          p.   cm.
     Includes bibliographical references (p.   ) and index.
     ISBN 0-435-08145-4
     1. Science--Study and teaching (Elementary)--United States.
  2. Science--Experiments.   3. Conjuring--United States.   4. Children-
-United States--Language.   5. Perception in children--United States.
  I. Title.
LB1585.3.S78   1997
372.3'5--dc21   96-49474
                                             CIP

Printed in the United States of America on acid-free paper
99 98 97 EB 1 2 3 4 5 6

To the fourth-, fifth-, and sixth-grade wizards
in towns and villages of the Green Mountains.
Without you, there would be no magic!

Contents

Preface

The seeing that is believing and the believing that is seeing make of the world we make for ourselves a haunted habitation. We are remarkably adept at believing what we have never seen—and at seeing what we have come to believe.

Wendell Johnson
"The Believing That Is Seeing"
from *Your Most Enchanted Listener*

Look at a rainbow, a large arc of colors in the sky, touching the mountain on your left and the meadow on your right. As you gaze, ask yourself the question: Is it really there?[1] More often than not, we take our senses for granted, believing without question in a real world outside ourselves, forgetting our own role in the creative process. However, if we think a bit about the rainbow, we soon realize it's the result of sunlight, the rain, and *our own vision!* It doesn't

---

1. The example of the rainbow is taken from Owen Barfield's *Saving the Appearances—A Study in Idolatry* (New York: Harcourt Brace, 1965). The first three chapters of Barfield's Book will be of interest to readers who want a deeper and more thorough explanation of the thoughts expressed in this preface.

exist without a lens, either in the eye of a beholder or behind the shutter of a camera. It appears and disappears "like magic," we might say.

The rainbow is like the sound of a tree we hear falling in the forest. If we aren't in the forest when it falls—if there are no ears anywhere in the forest—waves of compressing and decompressing particles of air pass from the fallen tree, throughout trunks, leaves, and branches, in a spherical wave. But there is no sound. Sound doesn't exist without an ear!

Though more difficult to keep in mind as we press our finger against the trunk of the tree, there are no unfelt solid things, only regions of particles, here far apart and there close together. The perceived world of butterflies, bird song and junipers is a world of representations of which we are an intimate part. Without our presence, of course, there is something there, but it is far from what we know and speak of as the world.

So if the rainbow "magically" disappears, we might ask: Where did it go? What do we mean by "magic"? What is the role of our senses in creating events and things we call real, and what is the role of language we use to describe them? What do we mean by "real," anyway? An event or thing that exists even if we don't? In this book, you will learn about some simple but magical changes of coins and string and cloth. As you read, ask yourself: If the touched coin vanishes, the cut string repairs itself, and one loop of cloth becomes two linked together, how many other things in the world might be, like the rainbow, less "real" than we suppose?

Both rainbows and vanishing coins can provoke children to ask such questions or, at least, to think about such things. As teachers we can make use of that provocation. Magic, like a rainbow, is created in the eye of the beholder. But how does this happen? What makes it work? What are we really seeing anyway?

Answering these questions provides a way for children to learn about how we see and how we use language to describe both thoughts and things—how we literally make SENSE of the world. This is how we come to know what we believe.

This is a book about magic, but it is much more than that. It is a book that closely examines how to help children experience and describe the world, how to experiment and ask questions about it, and how to make decisions about what is true and what isn't. It's about the science of magic.

Acknowledgments

Many people provided help during the writing of this book. Good friends and colleagues Glenda Bissex, Mary Jane Dickerson, Toby and Laura Fulwiler, Corinne Glesne, Willem Leenstra, Tony Magistrale, Jill and Rob Tarule, and Nancy Welch gave much needed critical and supportive comment. Ruth Kurtz took the photographs from which I drew the technical illustrations, and she was often there during magic shows to give a helping hand. Horace Puglisi and Teresa Robinson invited me into their classrooms to talk with them and their students about science and magic. They taught me much.

Thanks also to all the Vermont children who met with me in schools, libraries, and museums to talk about science and magic and about how we see the world. Their words and thoughts are the ground from which the dialogues in this book have grown. Finally, I thank my editors, Leigh Peake and Renée Nicholls, for their hard work, insightful comments, encouragement, and good humor. Without them, this book would not have been written.

Getting Started

Magic and Science in the Classroom

For there is a trickery about our senses that makes our seeing all suspect, save as we test it for the stray effects of fancy. And only far more testing than we think to do can make it fancy free.

Wendell Johnson
"Seeing What Stares Us in the Face"
from *Your Most Enchanted Listener*

  Thinking About Magic and Science

Cut a piece of string in half and it doesn't become a single piece again when you pick up the pieces. Push a needle into a balloon and the balloon bursts. These results aren't surprising. But what would you think if the halves of the string became whole again? Or if the needle passed right through the balloon to the other side and the balloon didn't burst?

When these things happen we call them *magic*—and they happen in magic shows. In *The Magical Classroom* you will learn how and why these and other magical appearances occur and about the scientific phenomena behind them. You and your students will learn how to become magicians, and in the process you will all learn a great deal about science, language, and perception.

Investigating magical effects and illusions and learning how to describe and present them provides a framework for helping children think very carefully about events that happen in everyday life. To learn about the natural phenomena involved in magic is to learn more clearly how to look at things, how to think about what you see, and how to know whether or not something might be true.

 ## Scientists and Magicians

Before we begin, we should know a bit more about what science is and what magic is. They are profoundly different, and they are carried out with opposite goals and purposes.

Most scientists would say they are trying to explore and understand how the world works so they can share that knowledge with each other and with us. Then we can all come to an agreement about what might be so and what might not. Scientists often search for what is hidden from our senses underneath the surface of things and for underlying causes of events in the everyday world we see, touch, and hear. They probe for what might be true. Knowing about science is essential for knowing about magic.

If they were candid, most magicians would say they are trying to entertain us by hiding the truth. They challenge us to discover what they have hidden. And we respond by trying to figure out the underlying causes of the magical effects and illusions we see. Like scientists, we search for the truth, for what might be hidden from our senses. Understanding physical science, as well as the science of perception and the science of language (semantics), is an important part of magic. Good magicians know a lot about science. If you want to *hide* the truth, it's useful to know how people come to know what they believe is true.

◉ Doing Science: "If, Then"

Suppose we visit a magician friend's house one evening. We might *pose the question:* Is she home? To answer our question we pose a *hypothesis. If* she isn't home and we ring the bell, *then* no one will come. This hypothesis is based on our past experience of our friend's behavior as well as our experience of doorbells and of what happens when you ring them. We can test it right away with a "ringing the bell" *experiment* and *observe the results:* No one comes to the door. We think, at first, we've answered our question. Our hypothesis is verified and we can come to a *conclusion:* No one is home. But is this conclusion logically valid? Not really.

That's because there are many reasons why she might not have come. For example, the bell might be broken. So we have a second hypothesis: *If* she isn't home and we bang on the door, *then* no one will come. We test this by banging on the door and observing that no one comes. She really seems not to be at home. We are now more certain of this. But can we be absolutely sure? Not at all.

What if she's sleeping and didn't wake up, or she's sick and doesn't wish to come? We could develop additional "if-then" hypotheses and test them with experiments: calling her on the phone, looking in the windows, checking the garage to see if her car is gone. If they are all verified (she doesn't answer the phone, she can't be seen by looking in the windows, and her car is not in the garage), we will at some point decide we've answered our question to a reasonable degree of certainty. She isn't home. We are probably—but not absolutely—correct.

Science never tells us whether the answer to a question is absolutely true, but we can test hypotheses until the answer is very highly probable. As we just noticed, there are many possible reasons why our friend might not have come to the door after we rang the bell. *One experiment isn't enough to answer the question.* Even several might not be sufficient. It's always possible someone borrowed her car and she turned off all the lights in the house, disconnected the phone, and is hiding in the basement practicing her magic tricks!

Scientists probe for truth in the same way that we tried to determine whether our magician friend was home, and they are well aware of limitations inherent in the scientific method. It NEVER leads to absolute truth, only to a high probability. *Science doesn't prove anything.*

⊙ Connecting Science and Magic

A hypothesis that has been verified millions of times with millions of experiments and confirming observations is called a *law*. A law is very, very probable indeed. No one seriously doubts that it is true. The "law of gravity" postulates an invisible attractive force exerted by the earth on objects near it, such as leaves, rain, people, buses and trains (this is really a simplified version of the law). Hypotheses of the type *"If* there is an invisible attractive force exerted by the earth on objects near it, *then* . . ." have been verified so many times that we no longer consider the force of gravity in terms of a hypothesis. Leaves fall from trees, rain falls from clouds and we don't have to worry about floating off into the sky. Gravity holds us all on the earth.

So what are we to make of our experience when we sit in an audience and a magician on stage floats an assistant ten feet up in the air over his head? Our life experience and our knowledge of gravity tell us it isn't possible, that it must be an illusion or trick. But how is it done? How is gravity defied? Why are we so intrigued by what we see? Why have we gone to see such a thing in the first place? Why can't we detect what is happening? To answer these questions we must consider how magic differs from science and also how it depends on our belief in the methods of science and the logic of cause and effect.

⊙ Doing Magic

Although science and magic have contradictory goals, the illusions of magic depend on what we know of science. That's because most of us model our thinking on something like the scientific method. We trust our cause-and-effect reasoning and our previous life experiences, as when we visited our magician friend who apparently wasn't home. She wasn't home BECAUSE she didn't come when we rang the bell. She wasn't home BECAUSE she didn't answer the phone. She wasn't home BECAUSE we couldn't see her through the window.

Magic gives rise to contradictions in our normal way of thinking, experiencing, and interpreting the world. In our mind we know that people don't float up in the air BECAUSE gravity holds them on the earth. We have a lot of experience with the law of gravity. We verify it each day of our life. In a performance of magic we are seeing something that contradicts both this law and our everyday experience. We are being asked to *suspend* our previous understanding of how the world works and our belief in causes and their resultant effects, at least temporarily. If gravity is holding us in our seat, why isn't it holding the magician's assistant to the floor? Can we suspend our belief in the law of gravity?

The joy of magic, of course, is that we don't really suspend our beliefs or normal way of thinking for very long, if at all. Most of us immediately try to fit the floating magician's assistant into our cause-and-effect world. It doesn't make sense. Few will just say "It's a trick" and leave it at that. In most of us, including almost all children, it provokes a tremendous desire to find out the truth about what is happening. And that curiosity is a tremendously powerful motivating force for learning. You want to learn how the magician levitates his assistant. You'll find out soon!

Motivating Students with Magic

Magic strongly motivates children to ask questions. What can I see and what can't I see? What is really happening? What is the cause of what I see? How can the impossible become possible? Such questions are the beginnings of scientific inquiry. Some causes of events are too fast to see or are too small, or are normally invisible or purposefully hidden (as in magic). To help your students discover the causes, you as a teacher have to help them think scientifically. You'll have to help them learn to ask critical questions about what they observe. You'll need to help them design and carry out experiments and look at the results very carefully. Most important, you will have to help them look for what might be under the surface or behind the scene. You'll need to help your students use the scientific method and carefully examine the language they use to describe things. When students learn to do magic and learn to understand the scientific principles and descriptive language behind effects and illusions, they begin to think more clearly and creatively. And they come to understand that what they see and what they don't are intimately connected to the descriptive language they use.

Magic, Language, and Perception

In both science and magic, asking questions about what we perceive and how we think about what we perceive is extremely important. Scientists and magicians are aware that what each of us sees is the net result of something *outside ourselves* (the world) and something *inside ourselves* (the structure of our eyes, nervous system, and brain). Each of us perceives and creates an individual, personal world. We use language to help us shape and represent this experience and to share it with others. And in sharing we come to agree about the collective world in which we coexist. The agreements we make are about the meaning of our *collective representations*, the symbols we use (words, pictures, etc.) to construct our shared world. These agreements make up what we, all together, call reality.

Understanding how we construct this reality is very important in teaching children about both science and magic and in teaching them about life in general. So how language is used is an important part of *The Magical Classroom*. This will be particularly apparent in the dialogues among students, which are a substantial portion of this book. These are constructed to direct, and to purposefully <u>misdirect</u>, in order to generate curiosity about the shared meaning of what is perceived and about what is real and what is not.

If you are asked to cut a piece of string in half and you cut it with a pair of scissors, you believe the string becomes two pieces. That's what you see, and the language of the request confirms it. But you will find out in the illusion "Amazing String" (Chapter 5) that this isn't so at all. If you are asked to press your finger down on a coin and you do it, you believe that you are touching the coin. That's what you see and feel. And it is what you are told. As you will find out in the illusion "Unbelievable Quarter" (Chapter 5), this isn't so either. In both these instances, what you think you do and what you actually do are two different things!

In magic, you are led by language, by what you think you see and feel, and by your past experience of simple things such as coins and string toward beliefs that are completely untrue. And language is critically important in creating these beliefs. The names of things, the meanings in the phrases "Cut this piece of string" and "Press your finger down on this coin," as well as the sensations you experience, lead you to construct a momentary reality that falls completely apart when the illusion is completed. This is real magic. And it is why

The Magical Classroom is filled with dialogue, and with names and meanings constructed in the context of the dialogue itself.

The descriptive language and agreements in these dialogues are as much a part of the effects and illusions as the physical objects that are manipulated. The language and the tentative agreements made by the observer (scientist) and performer (magician) create the temporary reality of the effect or illusion. The "cut" string magically becomes whole again. The coin you "touch" drops away from your finger through a solid barrier. Scientific explanations for the phenomena occurring and an analysis of the language describing them help you and your students see how language works to create what you come to believe and what you don't.

Magic honors dishonesty, with a wink of the eye, in order to entertain. An attempt is made to conceal, mislead, misdirect, mystify, deceive and confuse. And the fun, the real fascination, for the observer (scientist) is the attempt to use something like the scientific method of reasoning to discover the deception. Really good magic makes this very difficult indeed. Let's consider why this is so.

Levitating an Assistant: How It Works

On stage, the magician's assistant may appear suspended, but the law of gravity certainly can't be. There are many ways of "levitating" objects in front of someone who has only *visual cues*. What you see is often very misleading without other sensory input. Your past experience of the world and how it works tells you something must hold the assistant up, either from above or below, or from the side or back. You just can't see it. That's not quite true. Perhaps you aren't even seeing the assistant at all!

Here's how it looks. An assistant on stage lies down on a couch. The magician tells you he will make the assistant levitate, and then covers her with a large cloth. With appropriate hand movements and words, he commands the assistant to rise. Once the assistant is a few feet in the air, the couch is removed, and a command or motion is made to have the assistant rise higher, just above the head of the magician, who circles around the stage making appropriate remarks or movements. Finally, the magician grabs the front of the cloth with both hands and rapidly pulls it off. The assistant has disappeared—right in front of everyone's eyes.

Here's how it works. As soon as the assistant is reclining on the couch, a clear nylon mesh screen—permanently impressed with the body shape of the assistant—is lowered on four very thin black cords or threads by helpers offstage. The cords are already attached to each corner of the screen. The screen and cords are almost invisible because of the lighting and black background of the theater, and the molded screen is lowered to cover the body of the assistant entirely. As the screen is lowered, the magician directs the audience's attention toward the cloth he is picking up. Once on the assistant's body, the screen is sufficiently transparent so the assistant can be clearly seen through it.

The magician seems to cover the assistant with the cloth. Actually, he covers the mesh Then the assistant underneath the mesh slides into a hidden compartment in the couch. After the cloth-covered mesh is raised several feet with the cords, the couch is removed from the stage, taking the assistant with it. Everyone's attention is on the "floating" cloth-covered mesh, which has the exact shape of the assistant's body. For the audience, it has now become the assistant. Everyone believes it. By watching carefully, assistants off-stage can raise and lower the cloth covered mesh as directed by the magician's words or movements. As soon as the magician jerks the cloth off the mesh, it is rapidly pulled up to the ceiling, out of view of the audience. Again, the mesh is invisible because of the black background.

Even if you know how this illusion is done, what you perceive happening from a distance is quite different from what really happens. By careful concealment using color or lack of color (black cords, clear mesh, black background), specially constructed objects (body-shaped nylon mesh, hollow couch), and misleading, descriptive language, a person does seem to float and defy the law of gravity. Too many hidden things need to be combined in a cause-and-effect sequence to understand what is happening. It's a real whopper of a lie—and wonderful to see.

 ## What We See and What We Don't

In the illusion of the floating assistant, we make a mistake of perception. Such mistakes are quite common, even when we aren't purposefully misled, as in a performance of magic.

Walking down the street you look up ahead, see a friend, and yell "Hey Amber! Wait up for me." The girl turns around and you realize, with embarrassment, that it isn't Amber at all! What are we to make of such experiences? We've all had them. Consider a refrain from Lewis Carroll's "The Mad Gardener":

> He thought he saw a Banker's Clerk
> Descending from the bus,
> He looked again, and found it was
> A hippopotamus

While you won't mistake a bank clerk for a hippopotamus, it happens quite frequently in life that we see something that really turns out to be something else. The small "log" you see at the bottom of the lake moves and becomes a large fish! A reflection in the glass, which startles you, turns out to be yourself!

Examples of this sort, like mistaking the identity of a friend from behind, are most common for those things that reach our awareness through sight. What we see and our past experience combine to create an illusion. The floating magician's assistant is a classic example of such mistaken perception, created in a performance of magic. In understanding both science and magic, it is important to know how such misperceptions occur. How are we misled? And why does "I thought I saw" (your friend Amber, the log, the unrecognized reflection) change to "I found it was" (someone else, the fish, yourself) and sometimes it doesn't (the floating magician's assistant)? In other words, why are we able to discover the truth in some cases and not in others?

Let's go back once more to our place in the audience and look again at the floating assistant. Our eyes are all we have to help us discover what is happening. We are in a seat and can't move. The illusion may appear thirty feet in front of us. We aren't able to go up on stage and investigate, to look more closely behind, underneath, and above the assistant. We can't touch anything. And we can't see from the side, either. The rules in this illusion are very strict: Figure it out just by looking!

And besides that, we only get *one quick glimpse*. Once the levitation is over, it's over for good. There are no second looks, like when our friend "Amber" turned around, the "log" moved, or the "unrecognized reflection," on second glance, mirrored our own face.

So the floating assistant is a setup. It's created in a way that makes it impossible for us, as observers (scientists), to detect how it works. With careful direction from the magician, who uses language, lighting, movements, and special apparatus, and with only one very brief look, we miss entirely the cause of effects we think we see. We can make up hypothetical explanations in our heads (invisible wires and such), but we aren't allowed to test them. All the things we would want to do in a scientific inquiry are ruled out—no experiments, no further observations, no repetition! We have to hypothesize and draw conclusions from just one observation of the illusion and from our past experience.

Effects and Illusions

There are two types of magical phenomena described in this book. The first does not involve hiding objects or events, nor does it involve misdirection. It results from simple, natural processes or properties of materials that are not familiar or commonly apparent to most people. Electric fields, air pressure, and intermolecular forces fall into this category. However, the language used in dialogues describing such phenomena is purposefully misleading, focusing not on the natural process or phenomena, but on a fictitious "magical" explanation. This creates what we define as a magical *effect*. Effects included here are Curious Clips (Chapter 2), Weird Water (Chapter 2), Collapsing Can (Chapter 3), Rising and Falling (Chapter 4), and Upside Down (Chapter 6).

We define the second type of magical phenomena as a magical *illusion*, similar to the "floating assistant." These illusions depend very much on misdirection, hidden objects, deception—using both language and physical materials—and they work well only one time. They also often depend upon unusual properties of materials. Illusions included here are Incredible Balloon (Chapter 3), Surprising Spoon (Chapter 4), Amazing String (Chapter 5), Unbelievable Quarter (Chapter 5), and Crazy Cloth (Chapter 6).

The kinds of magic found in this book may be performed in the same way as the "floating assistant" illusion, allowing little experimentation, extended visual examination, or exploration. Or they may be scrutinized more closely with repetition and further study. Both techniques are valuable in helping children understand the nature of the scientific method and the limitations of a single, brief observation.

Which technique you choose should depend on the kind of magic involved. In the classroom, learning about the science behind magical *effects* is best achieved by repeating them over and over again, first by the performer and then by the observer, as students explore, hypothesize and do experiments together to try to understand what is happening. *Illusions* should be dealt with differently. Hypotheses, experiments and discussion focusing on illusions should initially be based on a single observation of the illusion. Only if no progress or understanding evolves should the illusion be repeated.

The second time you experience an illusion, you are looking at the presented objects and events with more educated eyes and hearing the spoken words with more educated ears. You become much more conscious of attempts to direct your attention away from some objects and toward others, and you become more wary of misleading language. When you see things a second time, you know the final outcome in advance. So you attend to things leading up to this outcome differently than you did the first time around, particularly in close-up magic. Many of the illusions in this book work like this. A cardinal rule for performing an illusion: Never do it more than once!

An important second rule in performing an illusion is: Never tell how it's done. All the curiosity, amazement, and motivation to discover what has happened vanish in an instant. And you take on some of the characteristics of a liar. That's why professional magicians always follow one illusion very quickly with a different one, and then another and another. There is no time for any extended critical thinking about what you are seeing. Students doing illusions will soon come to understand why they work very poorly with repetition, whereas scientific investigations require it. And in that revelation, the nature of magic and science will become clearer.

For both effects and illusions, the challenge for students is to try to understand what is happening by observing each one very carefully, asking critical questions, constructing hypothetical explanations, designing experiments to test these, observing results of the experiments and constructing logical explanations. It is important to consider some pedagogical techniques for doing this, but first let's consider the scientific phenomena that underlie the magic involved.

⊙ Scientific Phenomena Behind Magical Effects and Illusions

There are five main sections of the book, each focusing on different, important, scientific topics. Each section contains two effects or illusions that embody several important scientific concepts and principles which illustrate the phenomena.

Chapter	Effects and Illusions	Concepts and Principles
2. Invisible Attractions: Electrical Forces	Curious Clips: Tension at the Surface	surface tension, properties of water, atoms and molecules, chemical formulas, electrical and magnetic forces, soaps, oil, capillary action
	Weird Water: Collecting Electrons	electrons, positive and negative charges, static electricity, electrical forces, magnetic and gravitational forces, shocks, sparks, lightning
3. Conjuring with the Air: Gases and Atmospheric Pressure	Collapsing Can: The Weight of the Air	vaporization, condensation, states of matter, solids, liquids, gases, pressure of a gas, atmospheric pressure, volume of a gas, molecular motion, temperature
	Incredible Balloon: Through Thick and Thin	gas pressure, atmospheric pressure, molecular collisions, expansion and contraction, relation of gas pressure to movement and number of gas molecules
4. Magical Movements: Solids, Liquids, Gases, Mass, and Density	Rising and Falling: Dissolved Gases	atoms, molecules, formulas, carbonation, gases dissolved in water, density, mass, buoyancy, carbon dioxide, bubbles, pressure, water displacement, floating and sinking
	Surprising Spoon: Breaking Bonds	structure of solids, structure of liquids, changing a solid to a liquid, heat and atomic and molecular motion, how atoms bond to each other, breaking atom–atom bonds
5. Now You See It, Now You Don't: Physical Properties of Giant Molecules	Amazing String: Molecular Memory	twine, cellulose, molecular structure of giant molecules, polymers, monomers, properties of coils and twists

	Unbelievable Quarter: Seeing Through Molecules	translucency, transparency, crosslinking of polymers, stretching and relaxing of polymer molecules, small molecules vs. big molecules
6. Surface Sorcery: Topology and Chirality	Crazy Cloth: Topological Twists	topology, science of surfaces, properties of surfaces, meaning of *inside* and *outside*, symmetry and spatial relationships
	Upside Down: A Folding Inversion	properties of folds, front and back, up and down, symmetry and process, mirror images, identical and nonidentical

⊙ **Parts of Each Effect or Illusion**

Each effect or illusion is divided into five sections:

1. A *Dialogue* between performer and observer, which shows how the effect or illusion appears and highlights the language used to describe it.

2. A complete *Description* which includes *What You Need; How to Do It; How It Works;* and *Variations, Explorations, and Extensions.*

3. *What You See and What You Don't,* which summarizes which parts of the effect or illusion can be seen, which parts are hidden, and why.

4. *A Deeper Look,* which summarizes in greater detail, and at a higher level than *How It Works,* the science behind each effect or illusion.

5. *Questions to Draw and Write,* which provides avenues for further exploration and thinking about the effect or illusion, as well as leads for understanding the scientific concepts involved.

The Dialogue Section

This section contains a conversation between two students, one who is performing the effect or illusion (the magician), and the other who is an observer, or participating observer (the scientist). The dialogues help children understand how the attention and interest of an observer can be focused on some parts of an observed object or event and away from other parts.

We all see much that escapes our interest, and even more that escapes our attention. This must be so, for otherwise we would be too confused trying to pay attention to every sight and sound impinging on our eyes and ears. What we attend to, what captures our interest, and what we experience, depend in large part on what we are told to look at and care about.

The dialogues have been constructed in a way that puts the effects and illusions into the context of everyday life and language. In informal, conversational tones, they allow students to see how language can confuse and deceive, and how this—along with uncritical observation—can lead to misunderstanding.

There are many ways in which the dialogues may be used in the classroom. Children can analyze them, after learning about an effect or illusion, to find misleading language. They may review them prior to seeing an effect or illusion to guide them in observing more carefully. They may serve as prompts to get children to write their own dialogues or "patter" to go with an effect or illusion. You should use them in a way that best suits your classroom needs. Specific suggestions are provided in each chapter.

The Description

This section is the heart of each effect or illusion. *What You Need* provides a list of the items you'll need to gather. Most of these can be found in the kitchen, garage, bedroom, or bathroom. Occasionally you may need to purchase a small item at a grocery, hardware, stationery, or drugstore. *How to Do It* provides a detailed description of how to carry out the effect or illusion. It includes diagrams to help students see what is happening and what things should look like. *How It Works* contains a brief explanation, in scientific terms, of why the effect or illusion happens. *Variations, Explorations, and Extensions* summarizes related effects and illusions. It also contains additional writing, drawing, and science activities. These allow students to explore new ways of doing the effects and illusions so they can create their own personalized magic, as well as develop an understanding of how the effects and illusions work. In the process, their knowledge of the science and perceptual framework behind each effect will grow.

What You See and What You Don't

This section is devoted to two things:

1. *What is purposely hidden from the observer.* This focuses on how students can direct the observer's attention and interest away from a physical object or event with language, hand movements, misdirection, or simply by hiding something.
2. *What is hidden from the observer because it is too small or too fast to see or because it is normally invisible, such as air or an electrical field.* This section focuses on the properties and physical characteristics of normal objects that are unfamiliar—things that most people are unaware of or rarely attend to.

A Deeper Look

This section contains a more technical summary of the scientific principles underlying each effect or illusion. Here substantial real science—the chemistry and physics of everyday substances—is found. It provides a more extensive summary and background so that you may elaborate and extend the science behind each effect, coordinating it with your particular curricular or content goals. How much you choose to take from this section will depend on the ages of the children you are working with and the content of your regular science curriculum. It is written at a higher level than *How It Works* and often deals with descriptions of the submicroscopic structure and properties of materials or substances involved in the effect or illusion. Here you will learn about atoms and molecules, electrical fields, gases, liquids, polymers, and other interesting scientific phenomena that often underlie magic. Within this more extensive discussion you will be able to see how topics best relate to the regular science content of texts or materials you may be using.

Questions to Draw and Write About

This section includes a brief collection of writing and drawing exercises designed to extend the science and language concepts of each effect or illusion. Writing and drawing are critically important in helping children learn science. An old Chinese proverb says *I hear, I forget; I see, I remember; I do, I understand.* The last phrase, *I do,* should include writing as well as experimenting and observing, for all these activities involve active engagement and thinking about what is seen and heard. And the writing should be thought of as writing writ large: drawing pictures, making diagrams, writing numbers, and making lists. All of these are ways of representing thought on a page, taking it out of children's heads before it vanishes and placing it in front of their eyes so they can see what they understand and what they don't. Then rewriting and redrawing—a revision of thought—can occur. This is the very essence of learning.

Here, in the writing and drawing section of each effect or illusion, opportunities exist for implementing a variety of informal assessment strategies. Such assessment should focus not only on the knowledge of science concepts underlying effects and illusions, as evidenced by what students have written in their journals, but also on inquiry and problem solving skills that students develop in observing, explaining, designing experiments, and testing hypotheses—the bedrock of learning science. By paying careful attention to all of these areas, as evidenced by student writing and drawing in a journal, you can evaluate their level of achievement. This assessment effort should continue over time, and should always focus on how students come to understand both the process and content of their investigations.

 Magic and Science in the Classroom

Thoughts About Pedagogy

There are many ways this book can be used to teach children about science and magic, and to help them learn the skills of seeing things clearly, of asking questions and reasoning about what they see, and of coming to understand what they believe and what they don't. The particular techniques and pedagogy you use will depend on the size of your group, their ages and interests, and the learning and curriculum goals you have. The effects and illusions in this volume are quite appropriate for ages eight through fourteen. Whatever methods you choose, they should always focus on:

1. Careful observations and descriptions involving writing and drawing.

2. Asking questions and constructing hypothetical explanations for observed phenomena.

3. Careful experimentation, recording results in writing and drawing, interpreting them, and coming to a conclusion.

4. Careful attention to the various ways language is used to inform and to clarify, as well as to deceive and confuse.

◎ Techniques to Use

What follows are just a few examples of many techniques you might use. You should feel free to experiment with, modify, or alter these to fit your own particular teaching situation. Or you may wish to construct or invent your own methods.

In all cases, students should use a science journal or notebook for writing and drawing exercises. You should read and respond to children's writing and drawing regularly to motivate, support, and evaluate their efforts to learn. The hope is that the journal will contain not only lists of descriptions and directions for doing effects and illusions, but also a more complete record of children's scientific investigations about how they might work, what happens when they don't, and about the scientific principles and descriptive language that underlie them. Points one through four above emphasize critical and creative use of language in this way. The science journal or notebook provides a focus for this work and allows children to personalize their experiences with their own feelings and responses.

Teacher as Performer

If you are teaching a unit on gases and the atmosphere, for example, you may cast yourself in the role of the performer of Collapsing Can or Incredible Balloon, asking children to take careful notes and to pose questions in order to discover how each effect or illusion occurs. Be flexible and follow leads wherever they appear, connecting them to your regular curriculum and science content in a way that best suits your needs. For example, if you are doing a unit on solids, liquids and gases you can use Rising and Falling in addition to Surprising Spoon.

The first is an effect that illustrates gases dissolved in liquids, the nature of bubble formation, and buoyancy. The second is an illusion that illustrates properties of the solid state, what happens when solids are heated, and the relationship of heat to atomic or molecular motion.

The Deeper Look sections will help you see how to match your regular class content to an appropriate effect or illusion. The Questions to Draw and Write About sections will help you connect these to science content, and each dialogue will help you find ways to relate the effects and illusions to your regular classroom activities, particularly those focusing on language skills. It is impossible to predict beforehand exactly what will happen in any particular classroom with any one effect or illusion. That will depend on your teaching and curriculum needs and the particular level of your students. However, the emphasis should always remain on clear and credible observations and descriptions, careful writing and drawing, and critical and creative use of language and thoughtful explanations.

Try to provoke your students to ask questions, and to form explanatory hypotheses. You might also ask them to write out directions for experiments to test these hypotheses. For instance, after you show students Rising and Falling, you might ask them to make a list of reasons why they think the objects in the liquid are rising and falling. You could ask them to design a few possible experiments to test whether these possible reasons are correct or not. This leads to further experimentation, more descriptive writing, and so on. Additional leads to help you do such activities are provided in the Variations, Explorations, and Extensions section of each effect and illusion. These give suggestions for what experiments might be performed and for further experiments related to the effect or illusion. Student-centered explorations can be focused around these.

You might even wish to have an effect or illusion of the month, in which students focus on examining all aspects and extensions of that particular effect or illusion, relating it to their regular classroom content. For example, if you are studying the atmosphere, you might use the illusion Incredible Balloon to get things started. It provides a particularly exciting entry into the study of gases, gas pressure and the atmosphere.

Children as Performers (Magicians) and Observers (Scientists)

Instead of performing the effect or illusion yourself, divide the class into two groups, assigning a different effect or illusion to each group. Have each of the groups discuss their assigned illusion and practice performing it for each other. Share the dialogues with them and let them manipulate the materials. The two different groups should not share or communicate with each other at all during this phase of their work. It would be best to put them in different rooms or, at least, in different parts of the same room.

After an appropriate time period or perhaps the next day, assemble the whole class together with their materials. Divide them into pairs so that each half of the pair has learned about and practiced a different illusion or effect. They should be at a table or desk with each other, or at a bench where they have access to needed facilities (a faucet, sink, hot plate, or other apparatus) and the materials necessary for the illusion or effect they have studied and practiced.

Each half of the pair should now take turns being performer and observer. The performer presents the illusion to the observer, engaging him or her in a brief dialogue patterned after those in the book. Observers should take written notes and make diagrams or drawings of what they see. Observers should not have done any reading at all about the effect or illusion they are observing. This is a critical point.

After the effect or illusion is finished, ask the observer to use his or her notes and diagrams to write:

1. What did I see? (A complete description including both writing and drawing.)
2. How does it work? (A hypothetical explanation for what has been observed which could include both writing and drawing.)
3. What questions do I want to ask? (A list of questions and/or experiments he or she might wish to ask or perform to find out whether the explanation posed might be correct.)

The performer should write down a list of all the questions and comments he or she can remember that the observer has asked or made. A brief summary or assessment of the observer's reactions, surprise, or confusion should also be written down. The performer should then write whether he or she believes the effect or illusion "worked," along with comments about why or why not and a summary of how language was used to help carry it out. The performer should then attempt to answer any questions the observer wishes to ask.

The observer and performer should now share with each other what they have written and observed. The performer may now teach the observer how the effect works and help him or her perform it. Together, performer and observer should draft a written evaluation of the effect or illusion as magic. This should focus on:

1. What are we hiding when we do this effect or illusion, if anything?

2. What do we think is responsible for the effect or illusion? Is it misleading language or is it just something we weren't familiar with (a natural phenomena such as air pressure or an electrostatic charge)?

3. What surprised us about the effect or illusion?

4. What can we see that helps us understand what is happening?

5. How do we use language to mislead, confuse or deceive when we do the effect or illusion?

6. What other kinds of misleading language do we know of (e.g., advertising in magazines and on television)?

The summary might end with suggestions for altering, extending, or modifying any aspect of the effect or illusion in order to improve it. This might focus on the materials, the verbal presentation (descriptive and directive language), or the setting (the distance from performer to observer, the handling of materials, the lighting, the ability to keep something hidden, etc.). When the exercise is completed, each child should have had a chance to be a performer and an observer. Collaborative group work and sharing in the class as a whole may then be appropriate.

Observer Groups

You might instead wish to divide the class into groups of five or six. One member of each group will be elected or assigned the role of performer. The rest will be observers. For each observer group, you could ask some students to attend specifically to language use, others to visual observations, and still others to properties of the materials used. They all should write down their observations as the effect or illusion is performed.

All of the elected or assigned performers in the class will assemble together for an appropriate time to study the details of the effect or illusion, to practice doing it with each other, and to read the dialogues. They may also practice and prepare at home. The observers should get together in small groups and make a list of the things they will watch for and attend to when they observe any effect or illusion. For example:

1. Is someone lying to me?
2. Are things being hidden from me, or are there things that I can't see that are causing the effect or illusion?
3. What do I need to do, see, or ask to find out how the effect or illusion works?

Each performer then performs for his or her group of observers. Observers take notes and draw what they see. As a group, observers share their notes and drawings and make up a list of questions for the performer. Asking questions of the performer, who now should answer truthfully, they construct a hypothetical explanation and try to determine if it is correct. The observers now test their hypotheses directly by experimenting with the effect or illusion, along with the help of the performer.

National Science Education Standards

The Magical Classroom has been written to support classroom teachers interested in implementing the science content standards for grades five through eight in physical science elaborated by the National Research Council in its recent 1996 report.[1] The development of these standards was supported by the National Science Foundation, the U.S. Department of Education, the National Aeronautics and Space Administration, the National Institutes of Health, and the National Academy of Sciences. Consider the NRC grade 5-8 content standards for grades five through eight, and you will quickly see how *The Magical Classroom* can be used to support them.

---

1. National Science Education Standards, National Academy Press, 2101 Constitution Avenue, NW, Washington, DC 20418.

Content Standard A: Students Should Develop an Understanding About Scientific Inquiry and Develop the Abilities to Do a Scientific Inquiry

Inquiry begins with a question. All the effects and illusions in this book result in the immediate question: How does that happen? And magic is especially well suited to strongly motivate students to find an answer. That motivation is the driving force for the work involved in designing an investigation, gathering evidence, finding an answer to the question, and doing further investigation to support that answer—that is, *carrying out a scientific inquiry.* In order to find out how an effect or illusion works, students must learn to think critically and logically. In doing so, they will begin to understand the relationship between evidence and explanation. In investigating effects and illusions, students will learn to listen to and evaluate the explanations proposed by other students and to acknowledge different ideas and opinions. This will help them consider alternative explanations. All of these activities are essential components of the standards as described in the NRC report.

Content Standard B: Students Should Develop an Understanding of Properties and Changes of Properties in Matter, of Motions and Forces, and of Transfer of Energy

A glance at the right hand side of the table on pages 12–13 makes it quite clear that understanding all of these topics is an integral part of understanding and explaining the effects and illusions:

- *Properties of matter.* The properties of solids, liquids, and gases, and the concept of density are extensively explored in Chapters 3, 4, and 5.
- *Changes of properties in matter.* The concepts of vaporization, condensation, and change of state, as well as expansion and contraction of gases, are examined in Chapter 3. Changes in the solid state, changing from a solid to a liquid, and changes in polymers (stretching and contracting) are explored in Chapters 4 and 5.
- *Forces.* Electrical and magnetic forces, buoyancy forces, and bonding forces in solids and liquids are examined in Chapters 2, 4, and 5.
- *Motions.* Aspects of motion, symmetry, folding, and spatial relationships are examined in Chapter 6.

- *Transfer of energy.* Aspects of energy transfer (heat flow and its relationship to submicroscopic phenomena) are explored in Chapters 3 and 4.

◆◆◆

Now you have an understanding about the relationship between science and magic. And you can see how using magic in the classroom can help students learn the techniques, methods, and currently accepted content of physical science. Let's begin!

Invisible Attractions:
Electrical Forces

 ### Curious Clips: Tension at the Surface

◉ Dialogue

Paige: I'll bet if I put a box of paper clips in this full glass of water, they'll all go in. And the water won't spill over the side of the glass, either.

Amber: Maybe three or four will go in, but not a whole box!

P: You're wrong. I bet I can put the whole box in. That's seventy-five paper clips.

A: That would fill the whole glass with clips. The water will run over the side.

P: Will you do my week of dishes after dinner if I can fit seventy-five clips into the full glass of water?

A: Sure. But if some water goes over the side, then you'll do my share for a week *and* clean up my room for a month.

P: That's not fair!

A: I knew it. They won't fit in the glass unless the water goes over the side.

P: OK! I agree. I'll do your dishes and clean your room if I can't do it. Now watch.

[Paige slowly adds paper clips to the glass of water, one by one, as the girls carefully watch to see if water flows over the side of the glass.]

That's twenty of them.

A: If you add a few more, water will flow over the top. You'll never get to seventy-five.

[Paige keeps adding more and more, but the water doesn't flow over the top.]

P: There! I've added all seventy-five clips and the water didn't go over the side. I WIN! You've got to do my share of the dishes!

A: How is that possible? How can the clips and water fit in the same space?

P: *[Smiling]* Because they can.

◉ Description

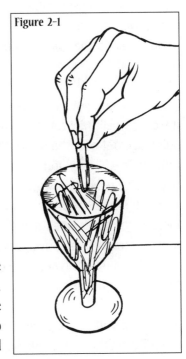

Figure 2-1

What You Need

1. A clear glass (one that is narrow at the bottom and wide at the top works best)

2. Water

3. A box of paper clips (you can substitute other items for the clips, such as pennies, small nails, or other things that will sink in water)

How to Do It

Fill the glass with water up to the top so that it reaches the edge but does not touch it. Drop in the clips one at a time, holding them vertically as you let them go, right above the center of the surface (Figure 2–1). Release them carefully so they don't make a splash when they drop in. You can add almost seventy-five paper clips to a medium-sized glass. They will go more than halfway up the glass before the water will go over the side. It looks amazing. How can so many clips fit into a full glass of water?

How It Works

If you look carefully at the top of the glass full of water and clips, you will see that the surface bulges out a bit. The water actually curves around from the edge of the glass as it goes toward the flat central surface.

A thin layer of water right at the top of the glass—the surface layer—pulls tightly together over the rest of the water, sort of like a skin. The skin is caused by the water inside the glass pulling down on the surface layer at the top. This "pulling down" is the force called *surface tension*.

Surface tension allows water to bulge out above the edge of the glass and keeps it from going over the side when you add the clips. The space taken up by the clips in the water is about equal to the space taken up by the water that bulges over the top of the glass.

Variations, Explorations, and Extensions

Try this experiment with different liquids, like vegetable oil, soda, vinegar, and Kool-Aid. Does it work as well? Mix some liquid soap into the water before you add the clips. Does the water still bulge out over the top of the glass as the clips are added? Does soap affect the surface tension "skin" of water? What can you say about the surface tension in oil compared to the surface tension in water?

Try different objects in the water instead of paper clips, such as pennies, nails, marbles, or any other small items that sink. Which gives the best effect by filling the glass the most before the water overflows?

Try different types of glasses with different surface areas at the top opening. Does a tall, narrow glass work as well as a conical glass (very small at the bottom and wide at the top)?

Can you float a paper clip on the surface of a full glass of water? If you carefully place a clip flat on the surface, it should be easy to float it. If you put it in end first, it won't work. Why is that?

⊙ What You See and What You Don't

When paper clips are going into the glass of water, they seem to be taking up a lot more space than they really are. If you could take all the clips and melt them to a liquid, you would see that they don't take up much space. The *volume* of the clips, the amount of three-dimensional space they take up, is much less than it appears to be. You cannot easily determine an object's volume with just a quick look.

The clips are really just thin wires bent around on themselves, all in a jumble. Water surrounds them on all sides. After seventy-five clips are added to the glass, the volume of the water bulging out at the top of the glass is about the same as the volume of the clips added. This doesn't seem to be the case because the bulging volume of water is transparent and relatively thin, like a piece of glass. The clips are dark and jumbled, all in a mass. Using just vision alone, we perceive that the clips take up more space than they really do. The surface of the water before the clips are added looks almost the same as after they are added, but this is not the case. Looking quickly isn't sufficient to see what is really so.

The effect is enhanced even further because of something called *capillary action,* an attraction of the glass to the water at the very edge. The water in the glass before the clips are added does go up to the top, but the water surface near the edge curves up the inside of the glass. The *center* of the surface is not this high. This is because of capillary action. There is no glass in the center of the surface, so it is lower. So before the clips are added, the surface is slightly concave, and after the clips are added, it is slightly convex (Figure 2–2). The difference between these two is more than enough space to allow water to bulge out from the added clips.

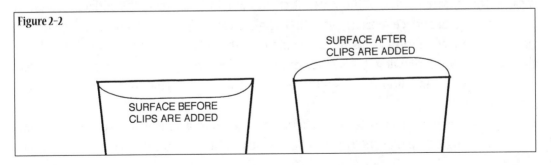

Figure 2–2

SURFACE AFTER
CLIPS ARE ADDED

SURFACE BEFORE
CLIPS ARE ADDED

◎ A Deeper Look

Water is composed of a very, very large number of water *molecules*. Each molecule contains two hydrogen atoms and one oxygen atom (two H's and one O). The formula for a water molecule is written as H_2O.

In a water molecule the H atoms are partially positive and the O atom is partially negative. The attractive force between one molecule of water and another results from the positive hydrogens of one molecule attracting

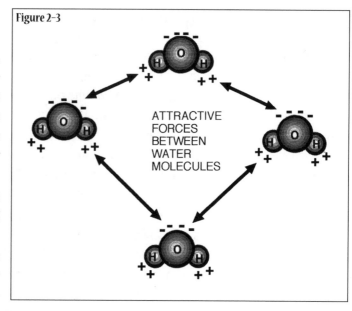

Figure 2-3

ATTRACTIVE FORCES BETWEEN WATER MOLECULES

the negative oxygen of another (Figure 2–3). While this attractive force is similar to the force exerted by a magnet pulling an iron nail toward it, it is an *electrical* force rather than a magnetic one.

A molecule of water in the middle of a glass of water is subject to attractive electrical forces in all directions from all the molecules around it. But a water molecule at the surface of a glass of water experiences only the attractive force from those molecules beneath it (Figure 2–4). This results in a net *inward force* on the surface layer of molecules. This surface force is called the *surface tension* of the water. It creates a tight "skin" over the surface.

Because of surface tension, water in the glass can bulge out beyond the edge of the glass. The surface tension keeps it from going over the side as the clips push it out of the glass. Instead of overflowing, the surface of the water at the top of the glass starts to curve from the edge, up and around toward the center of the surface. The "skin" holds the water in this shape.

Surface tension also forces single drops of water into a spherical shape. You can see this when a single drop of water sits on a flat surface. Sitting drops tend to curve over and be round on top. Other liquids have smaller attractive forces between their molecules, and drops of these liquids on a flat surface are not spherical (nail polish remover, for example). They spread out in a thin layer.

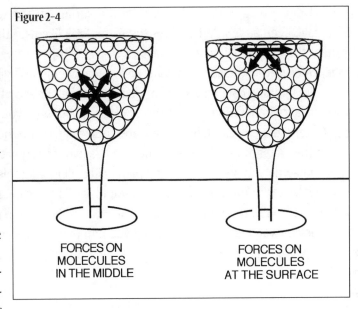

Figure 2-4

FORCES ON
MOLECULES
IN THE MIDDLE

FORCES ON
MOLECULES
AT THE SURFACE

The tight "skin" of water molecules formed on the surface of water by surface tension is strong enough so you can float a paper clip on the surface if you carefully lay it down flat. This is how bugs called "water striders," as well as some other insects, can walk on water. If you look carefully, you can even see their feet making a "dent" in the surface layer.

⦿ Questions to Draw and Write About

Write out a conversation similar to the one between Paige and Amber, in which you are the one adding something to the glass of water and a friend is observing. In your conversation, add something besides paper clips. Can you write a conversation that more effectively surprises Amber than Paige did? What kind of language would you need to do it?

In your own words, write out a definition of surface tension. Then go to the library and find some chemistry or physical science books and a dictionary. Does your definition seem similar to the definitions you read? Could you improve upon the dictionary or chemistry or physical science book definitions?

Pretend you have access to a super-powerful magnifying device that allows you to view water molecules. Draw what you think you might see if you used this device to view the surface layer of water bulging out from the top of the glass of water and clips.

Draw a diagram (a side view) of the surface of the water in the glass after all the clips have been added. What does the water look like near the edge of the glass compared to near the center? Fill a small glass to the very top with vegetable oil and look near the edge. Does it look the same as water near the edge of a full glass of water?

Imagine you are a paper clip floating on the surface of a container of water. Write a short paragraph describing what this is like. Explain what you feel is keeping you from sinking. Pretend the clip can talk to the water molecules all around it. What would it say? What would the water molecules say to the clip? Use your imagination.

Imagine you are one of many paper clips all in a jumble in a glass that is filled to the top with water. Write down what you would say to the clips around you. How do you feel? Where are you in the jumble of clips? At the top, bottom, or middle? What are you doing in a glass of water, anyway? Normally you clip papers together, but now you're sitting in a glass of water. Speaking as a clip, explain what's going on.

 Weird Water: Collecting Electrons

Dialogue

Bobby: Hey José, want to see me bend some water?

José: What do you mean, bend? You can't bend water.

B: It bends when I squirt the hose up in the air doesn't it?

J: So what? It's just falling back to the ground.

B: I can bend it sideways.

J: What do you mean, sideways?

B: Take this ballpoint pen and use the pen tip to punch a small hole in the center of the bottom of this paper cup.

J: What's that got to do with bending water?

B: Just do it José, and then I'll show you.

J: OK. OK. But . . .

B: Now hold your finger over the hole in the bottom, fill the cup with water, and hold it over the sink.

[José does this.]

J: OK. Now what?

B: Now I'm going to rub this balloon on my sweater. You take your finger off the hole and let a stream of water come out of the hole into the sink.

J: The water is running out. But it isn't bending.

B: Watch what happens when I bring the balloon near the water as it runs out.

J: That's really interesting. The stream of water is bending toward the balloon. How come it does that?

B: It's a magical balloon. I forgot to tell you.

J: No it isn't. It's a regular old balloon.

B: Then why does it work?

J: I don't know. You tell me.

◉ Description

What You Need

1. A paper cup

2. Water

3. An inflated balloon

4. A ball point pen

5. A faucet and sink

6. A sweater

How to Do It

This effect is much easier to do with a friend. It's also more fun if the observer helps you do it. Use the ballpoint pen to punch a hole in the center of the bottom of the paper cup.

It should be a very small hole, as perfectly round as you can make it. Holding your finger over the hole, fill the cup with water. Then you or the observer should rub the balloon rapidly on a sweater five or six times.

Now, hold the cup well above the sink and take your finger off the hole. A narrow stream of water will run out of the hole into the sink. Have your friend bring the just-rubbed balloon near the middle of the stream and watch the water carefully. Wow!!! The water bends (Figure 2–5). You are bending water with an invisible force coming from the balloon! What could be happening?

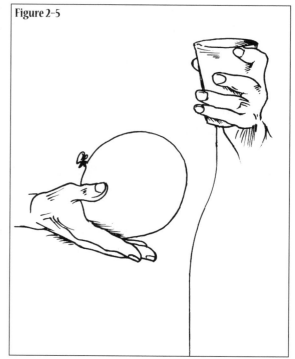

Figure 2-5

How It Works

When you rub a rubber balloon against something with lots of small strands, threads or yarn (such as your hair, fur, or a sweater), it acquires *electrons* (small, negatively charged particles). These charged particles are picked up by the rubbing motion, and this creates a negative charge on the balloon.

This charge exerts an invisible "pulling" force on other things that have fewer electrons than the balloon. Such things have a positive charge relative to the balloon. The force is similar to the magnetic force that attracts iron to a magnet, but is electric rather than magnetic. The stream of water consists of water molecules that have positive and negative ends (see A Deeper Look, pages 34–36). When the negatively charged balloon comes near the stream, the water molecules turn themselves so that their positive ends (the H atoms) are facing the negatively charged balloon. As this happens, the attractive, electrical force between the balloon and water causes the stream to bend.

Variations, Explorations, and Extensions

There are all kinds of variations you can try. Instead of plain water, you could try salt water or sugar water. Do these bend more or less?

You could also try different liquids, such as oil, vinegar, soda, or milk. Try rubbing different objects instead of a balloon. Try a plastic pen or a plastic spoon. You can also try rubbing the objects on different things. For instance, you could try rubbing an empty plastic soda bottle on a carpet.

Which items and liquids work the best? Which don't work at all? If you punch two holes in the cup and two streams of water run out, do both streams bend the same way as one does? If you use a long, skinny balloon instead of a round one, you can bring it near the stream in two different ways, near the end and near the middle of the balloon. Does each bend water the same amount? Can you explain the result in terms of the amount of negative charge on the various parts of the balloon?

Will tissue paper be attracted to a rubbed balloon? Try an experiment and see. Is the tissue positively charged or negatively charged? Try combing your clean, dry hair rapidly and repeatedly with a comb. Will salt particles poured on the table from a salt shaker jump up to your comb if you hold it near the salt? If they do, explain why.

What You See and What You Don't

The charged particles that build up on the balloon are completely invisible. They are much too tiny to see, even with the most powerful microscope. Nevertheless, the attractive force, or "pulling," that they exert causes a visible change in the falling stream of water. The water falls straight down from the cup because the only force affecting it (when the balloon isn't there) is the force of the earth's gravitational field. This force holds you on the ground. It keeps everything that isn't attached to the earth from floating into the air. And it pulls water out of the cup down into the sink.

This gravitational force is invisible. We live our lives under its constant influence and become used to it. When you throw a ball up in the air, it always comes back down. Fruit falls from trees, rain falls from the sky, and when you jump up, you come back down—just like the ball. Since we grow up with the earth's gravity all around us all the time, its effects aren't surprising. It's the way things are.

When we observe objects in the absence of gravity, we are amazed and entertained. In the space shuttle, for example, water floats in spherical globes and astronauts float half way between the floor and ceiling. We are also sometimes amazed, or at least amused, by other forces in addition to gravity. There are two of these that we can experience easily: electrical forces and magnetic forces. Most of us have had fun playing with magnets and are fascinated by the pull of one magnet on another, or on a piece of iron.

Direct experiences of electrical forces are less common, except when we take clothes from the dryer and they "cling" to us. Or when our recently washed and dried hair, on a very dry, winter day, jumps up to the comb held near it. These movements of hair and cloth are caused by electrical forces that result when charged particles accumulate on clothes in the dryer or on our hair. Can you imagine how products like Cling Free, small squares of cloth that are added to the clothes in the dryer, stop the buildup of charge on your clothes?

Bending a stream of water with a balloon that has been rubbed on a fibrous surface results from a force similar to the force that causes clothes to cling to us when they first come out of the dryer. The constant tumbling in the dryer rubs particles on the cloth, similar to your rubbing the balloon on your sweater. This force is not a gravitational force, but an electrical force. All the forces—gravitational, magnetic and electric—(more correctly called *force fields*) are invisible. They cannot be seen. All you can see is the effect of them on objects.

◉ A Deeper Look

All substances are composed of atoms, which are made of three kinds of particles:

1. electrons, which are negative;
2. protons, which are positive;
3. neutrons, which are neutral (Figure 2–6).

The protons and neutrons are very large compared to the very tiny electrons. However, they are still much too small to see, even with the most powerful microscope. The negative electrons are much smaller and very, very light. When you repeatedly rub a balloon or piece of plastic on fibrous material such as a wool sweater, electrons come off of molecules and stick to the balloon. If enough of them do this, they build up a *negative charge* on the balloon.

This negative charge will be attracted to anything that has less negative charge on it. For example, if you put the rubbed balloon near your clean, dry hair, the strands of hair

Figure 2-6

REPRESENTATION OF A TYPICAL ATOM (OXYGEN)

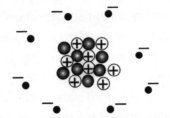

⊕ PROTON WITH POSITIVE CHARGE

● NEUTRON WITH NO CHARGE

– ELECTRON WITH NEGATIVE CHARGE

THE PROTONS AND NEUTRONS ARE IN THE NUCLEUS OF THE ATOM. THE ELECTRONS ARE OUTSIDE THE NUCLEUS.

IN A REAL ATOM THE ELECTRONS ARE MUCH SMALLER THAN SHOWN. THE MASS OF THE ATOM IS ALMOST ENTIRELY IN THE NUCLEUS.

IN A NEUTRAL ATOM
THE NUMBER OF PROTONS = THE NUMBER OF ELECTRONS.

jump out toward the balloon and touch it. Relative to the balloon, those strands have fewer extra electrons. They have a *positive charge* relative to the balloon. There is an attractive force between objects that have a positive and negative charge. This attractive force results from what is called an *electrical field.*

Many different kinds of objects can acquire positive and negative charges. If they are near each other, movement of the objects may be observed. If they are held rigidly in place, a force of attraction can be felt between them. If enough electrons build up on an object, they can often jump from it to a positively charged one. A lightning bolt is an example of extra electrons traveling between a cloud and the earth.

You can sometimes build up electrons on your body when you walk across a wool carpet on a dry, winter day. When you put your finger near a metal object on the ground or floor, the electrons can sometimes jump from your body and create a small spark. You feel this as a shock. The electrical charge that builds up on your body as you cross the carpet, or that builds up on the balloon when it is rubbed, is called *static electricity*. These are electrons that do not move (they are static). They are just sitting on you, or on the balloon. This is quite different from electrons flowing in a wire or through the filament of a light bulb. That is an example of an *electrical current* (the electrons are moving).

When a rubbed balloon with extra electrons and a negative charge is held near a small stream of water running from a hole in a paper cup, the stream has a positive charge relative to the balloon and is attracted to it. This attractive force causes the stream to alter its course (Figure 2–7).

When the balloon isn't there, the only force acting on the water is the earth's gravity, so it flows straight down. When the balloon is brought near, an additional force—an *electrical force of attraction between the negative balloon and positive stream*—is exerted. Instead of flowing straight down, the stream of water bends toward the balloon.

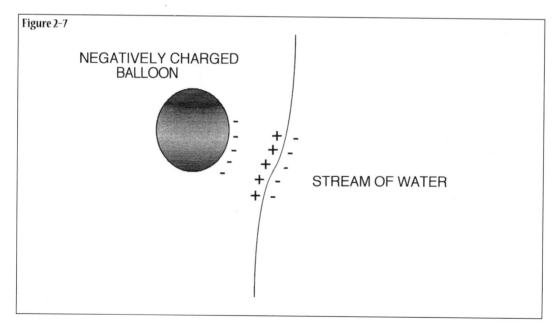

Figure 2-7

NEGATIVELY CHARGED BALLOON

STREAM OF WATER

⊙ Questions to Draw and Write About

How would you define *static electricity?* Why are the electrons on the balloon characterized by the term static? Look up the word *static* in the dictionary. What does it mean, and how does it apply in the term *static electricity?*

Draw a magnified picture of what you think is going on when the balloon comes near the stream of water. For purposes of illustrating your picture, assume an electron is a small, spherical particle. Double-headed arrows (◄────────►) are sometimes used to represent an attractive electrical force between positively and negatively charged objects.

As you draw your picture, remember that charged particles are either positive (+) or negative (-), and that positive and negative particles attract each other. In your picture, put negative particles on the balloon and positive ones on the stream of water.

Give an example of another invisible force which can "bend" a stream of water. Can you "bend" a stream of water with a magnet? Why or why not? Can you design an experiment to check this out? When you squirt water up in the air from a hose, what force causes the water to curve around and drop back down to the ground? What would happen if you could squirt water "up in the air" from a hose in the space shuttle? Does the word *up* have the same meaning in the space shuttle as it does on the surface of the earth? What about the word *down?*

Go back and look at the diagram of a water molecule (page 28). Does the molecule have a net negative charge or a net positive charge (i.e., does a single molecule have more + charges on it than - charges)? Which part of the water molecule, as shown in that diagram, would be attracted to a negatively charged balloon, the oxygen or the hydrogen atoms?

Look at the picture of the oxygen atom and pretend you are an electron in this atom. Describe what you would see and feel. What forces are acting on you? Describe them. Now pretend you are a proton (a much larger, positive particle) in the nucleus of the oxygen atom. Now describe what you would see and how you would feel. What forces are acting on you?

Imagine you are an electron sitting in an atom, in a molecule, in your living room carpet. Someone is rubbing a balloon on top of you and you loose your grip on the carpet and become attached to the balloon. Draw a cartoon picture of what is happening from your point of view. Put a funny caption on the cartoon describing what is happening.

Imagine being a water molecule in a stream of water running from the faucet. You have a positive end and a negative end. A balloon with negative electrons is brought near you. Describe how you are affected by this. How do you react?

Conjuring with the Air

CHAPTER 3

Gases and Atmospheric Pressure

 ## Collapsing Can: The Weight of the Air

◉ Dialogue

Amber: José, I've just finished a soda, and I can make the can collapse and crumple without touching it with my hands.

José: Sure, you can just ask Mom to drive over it with the car!

A: No, I don't mean like that. I can do it right here in the kitchen.

J: So you'll step on it.

A: No. I don't mean that way.

J: So what do you mean?

A: While I'm holding it with the barbecue tongs, it will collapse and crumple all by itself.

J: You're not going to squeeze it?

A: No, I'm not. But I'll need the kitchen stove and a bowl of ice water.

J: You're going to try and melt the can on the stove? It won't work, Amber.

A: No, of course not. Now you fill up the bowl with ice and then add some water to the top, while I turn on the stove.

J: OK! Here's the bowl of ice water.

A: Now watch while I heat the can for a second over the stove. I'm going to hold it with the tongs because it'll get hot.

J: OK, I'm watching. Nothing's happening.

A: Be patient, José. It's going to take a few minutes.

[Amber holds the bottom of the can over the burner for a minute until steam is rising from the open hole in the top of the can.]

J: It's steaming, but I don't see it crumpling at all.

A: Gee whiz, wait a second. Watch me now.

[She removes the can from the stove using the tongs and quickly turns it upside down and lowers just the top into the ice water in the bowl. There is a loud bang.]

J: Wow! What happened? Look at that can.

A: Obviously the can is completely mashed, crushed, crumpled, and flattened.

J: But what did it?

A: Maybe I crushed it with the tongs?

J: No way. It happened too fast, and with a loud bang.

A: So you tell me what happened.

J: But I don't know!

⊙ Description[1]

What You Need

1. An empty aluminum soda can

---

[1] THIS EFFECT SHOULD BE DONE WITH AN ADULT!

2. A bowl of ice and water

3. A hot plate or other source of heat

4. Tongs

How To Do It

Put about half a teaspoon of water into the empty soda can and set it on a burner or hot plate at low heat. *Have an adult help you do this!* Wait for a minute until you can hear the water boiling in the can and steam is rising from the hole in the top.

Grab the steaming can near the bottom with the tongs and quickly invert it over the bowl of ice water. Plunge just the top of the can into the bowl of ice water. Don't be startled by the very loud bang you will hear as the can completely collapses. The sides are mashed into each other! (See Figure 3–1.)

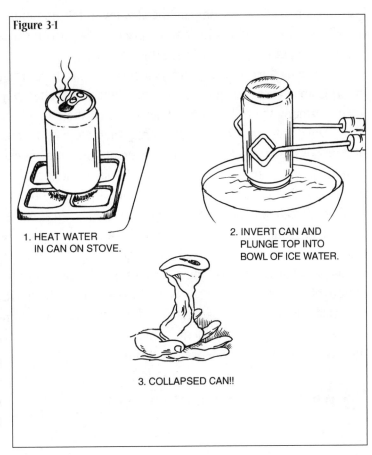

Figure 3-1

1. HEAT WATER IN CAN ON STOVE.

2. INVERT CAN AND PLUNGE TOP INTO BOWL OF ICE WATER.

3. COLLAPSED CAN!!

How It Works

When you heat the can with a little water in it, the water boils and turns to steam. The steam pushes all the air out of the can. When you plunge the upside-down can full of steam into the ice water, all the steam condenses back to water, leaving the can with no air inside. The can now contains a *vacuum* (no air or steam), and the atmospheric pressure on the outside pushes the sides of the can in on themselves. The loud bang is the result of the aluminum sides smashing into each other as the can collapses.

Variations, Explorations, and Extensions

Try different-sized cans. Compare the effect with tall aluminum cans and shorter ones. Will the effect work if you just heat an empty can? See if you can reduce the amount of water you need to put in the can to make the effect work.

Examine the crushed can very carefully. Can you see where the sides are touching each other? Compare a series of cans. Are they all identical after they collapse, or do you see differences among them? If you see differences, what are they?

See if steel cans behave differently than aluminum cans. Some juice cans are made of different metals with a coating to prevent corrosion. These may be a bit stronger than aluminum soda cans. Punch a dime-sized hole in the top of the can. Steel cans take longer to cool, so don't touch the cans too soon. See if they behave differently when they are filled with steam and plunged into the ice water.

The same effect can be obtained if a metal can with a screwtop is heated full of steam to drive the air out of it and is then quickly sealed with a cork or the screwtop. Cleaning products and waxes often come in such cans. Your parents or teacher should wash these out thoroughly with soap and lots of water before you use them. NEVER use any screwtop metal cans that have contained flammable materials! Also, *have an adult help you so you do not burn yourself!* In these experiments, it may take a few seconds before the cans collapse because there is no ice to help condense the steam.

◉ What You See and What You Don't

In this effect you really see everything that is possible to see. What no one can see (including you) is what really causes the can to collapse. Living on the surface of the earth we are all under the very large pressure of the atmosphere. This pressure is caused by the mass of invisible air that continues for miles above us. We can't see this air. And that's a good thing too, because otherwise we wouldn't be able to easily move about and know where we are going. What most of us are also completely unaware of is the massive pressure this air exerts on everything at the surface of the earth, including you, everyone else, and soda cans! That's no problem for a can full of soda, air, or steam. But it matters a lot if the can has absolutely nothing inside it.

Though invisible, the pressure of the air has a profound influence on how things behave. This is quite apparent in this experiment. The steam inside the can doesn't seem to be holding the sides of the can apart against the pressure of the air outside it, but if you cover the can and the steam changes back into liquid water, which has a much smaller volume than steam, the effect of the atmosphere is dramatic and quite visible. Since there is almost nothing at all left inside the can to hold the sides apart against the atmospheric pressure, the can collapses.

It appears as if the can collapses and crumples all by itself. But of course this isn't so. The use of the phrase *all by itself* is a very misleading use of language. Air is invisible, and the effect of its pressure upon us, as well as upon the can, is never really part of our awareness. This massive weight of the air presses down on the empty can and mashes it almost flat! It didn't collapse by itself at all.

If there were no atmospheric pressure of air we would find it impossible to live, even if we didn't need to breathe. The pressure of the atmosphere keeps our blood from boiling and our eyes in our heads, and in general, it keeps us in "good shape." We depend on this pressure to go about our everyday lives. When astronauts go into outer space (which is also a vacuum just like the one inside the can just before it collapses), their space capsules need to carry an atmospheric pressure inside. And these capsules must not leak. When astronauts go for space walks they must carry their own atmospheric pressure inside their space suits.

◎ A Deeper Look

We all live under a sea of invisible air that exists miles above us. Though we are not consciously aware of it, this air exerts a pressure of about fourteen pounds on every square inch of the earth's surface (Figure 3–2).

The pressure drops at higher elevations, such as the top of a mountain, since there is less air above the surface at the top of a mountain than in the valley below it. If you blow up a balloon and seal it in the valley, it will have a certain volume. This volume results from

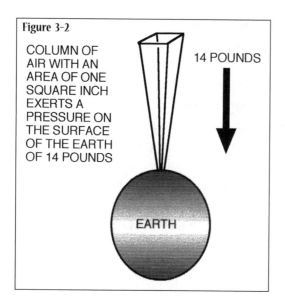

Figure 3-2

COLUMN OF AIR WITH AN AREA OF ONE SQUARE INCH EXERTS A PRESSURE ON THE SURFACE OF THE EARTH OF 14 POUNDS

14 POUNDS

EARTH

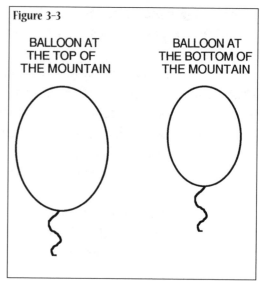

Figure 3-3

BALLOON AT THE TOP OF THE MOUNTAIN

BALLOON AT THE BOTTOM OF THE MOUNTAIN

air inside the balloon pushing out against the inner walls and against the outside air pressure that is pushing on the outer walls. If you take a filled, sealed balloon from the valley to the top of a mountain, its volume will increase because the air pressure on the outside of the balloon is less on the mountain top. The gas inside can then stretch the balloon a bit more and make it larger (Figure 3–3).

The relationship between air pressure and volume can be expressed mathematically. At a constant temperature, the pressure multiplied by the volume is equal to a constant:

$$P \times V = a\ constant$$

This means that if the pressure increases, the volume of gas in a container that is flexible enough to change its volume (e.g., a balloon or a cylinder with a piston) will diminish. If the pressure decreases, the volume will increase (Figure 3–4). This is known as *Boyle's Law*, after the scientist who first studied the relationship between gas volume and pressure.

In the Collapsing Can experiment, the air inside the open can has the same pressure as the atmospheric pressure outside it. If you add a bit of water to the can and then heat it,

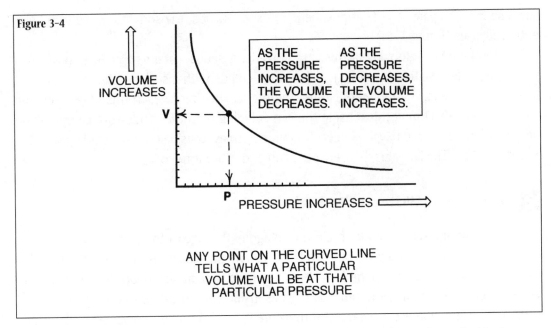

Figure 3-4

VOLUME
INCREASES

AS THE   AS THE
PRESSURE   PRESSURE
INCREASES,   DECREASES,
THE VOLUME   THE VOLUME
DECREASES.   INCREASES.

V

P   PRESSURE INCREASES ⟹

ANY POINT ON THE CURVED LINE
TELLS WHAT A PARTICULAR
VOLUME WILL BE AT THAT
PARTICULAR PRESSURE

it will boil and change to water vapor. Water vapor is a gas, and when it forms inside the can, it pushes all the air out.

The gaseous form of water takes up much more space (volume) than the liquid because molecules of water vapor (gaseous water) are moving much faster than molecules of liquid water. Molecules are also much farther apart from each other in gaseous water than in liquid water. The air in the can is pushed out by the fast-moving, far-apart molecules of water vapor, so all the air in the can is expelled.

When the can is full of hot water vapor, it can be grasped with a pair of tongs and turned upside down. The vapor won't easily come out because the air outside the can holds it in. When the top of the upside-down can is immersed in ice water, two things happen.

First, the can is sealed off. No air can get in anymore. Second, the water vapor inside the can is rapidly cooled. When it cools, the vapor condenses back into liquid water, which takes up much, much less volume. Since no air can get in the can, the pressure inside goes way down. At the same time, the pressure of the atmosphere pushes on the side of the aluminum can at more than fourteen pounds per square inch. Since the pressure inside the can is so low compared to the atmospheric pressure outside, the soda can rapidly and violently collapses (Figure 3–5).

Another way of looking at this is to consider gaseous water as a collection of small moving particles (water molecules). When they collide with a surface, they exert a pressure. The more gas, the more collisions, the higher the pressure. In this case, there are fewer gaseous water molecules inside the can colliding with the inside surface than there are gaseous nitrogen and oxygen molecules (air molecules) outside the can colliding with the outside surface. The latter crash against the can and cause it to collapse.

◎ Questions to Write and Draw About

Draw a picture of a sealed can with air in it. Magnify the size of the air molecules moving about inside the can and draw what you think you might see as they crash into the inside walls. Draw what you think the molecules of air outside the can would look like as they crash into the outside walls. If the number of crashes inside and outside are equal over a period of time, the can will not collapse. But if there are fewer molecules crashing into the inside

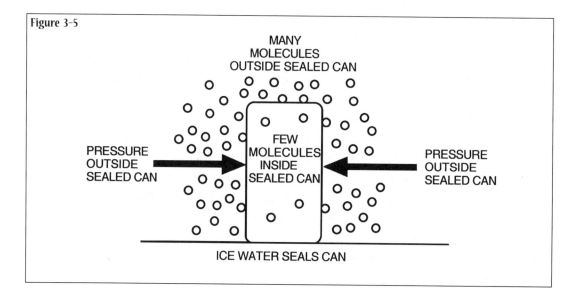

Figure 3-5

MANY
MOLECULES
OUTSIDE SEALED CAN

PRESSURE
OUTSIDE
SEALED CAN

FEW
MOLECULES
INSIDE
SEALED CAN

PRESSURE
OUTSIDE
SEALED CAN

ICE WATER SEALS CAN

walls than the outside walls, the outside crashes will push the walls in. Draw what you think you might see as this happens.

Examine the dialogue between Amber and José very carefully. At what point is Amber misleading José? Make a list of her misleading statements. Did Amber tell José that there was a little water in the can before she began heating it? Why or why not?

Write a story or draw a cartoon strip that incorporates the kinds of changes that happen when the can collapses. Draw a single cartoon picture of a surprised observer watching the can collapse. Put a funny caption below the cartoon.

Imagine you are an empty aluminum soda can going through the effect Collapsing Can. Write a story (from the can's point of view) describing all the changes that are happening to you. Describe what it feels like when the steam inside you condenses and the pressure on your outside becomes much greater than the pressure on your inside. What are you experiencing as you collapse?

Imagine you are a water molecule inside the can being heated on the hot plate. Write a short description of what happens when you and all your water molecule friends change from liquid water into steam. Then tell what happens when you are cooled in the bowl of ice and change back to liquid again.

What happens when you try this effect with a very strong steel can, which *won't* collapse? Why does water from the bowl push up into the can? Can you explain what is happening? Draw a picture that shows what you see.

 Incredible Balloon: Through Thick and Thin

 Dialogue

    Amber: I'm going to poke this balloon with a sharp knitting needle.
    Bobby : Stop it Amber, you'll pop it!
    [Bobby starts to put his fingers in his ears.]
    A: No, I won't.

B: Of course you will. Cut it out. Why are you wasting a balloon?

A: I'm not wasting it. It won't pop.

B: That's crazy. You're going to push a needle into a balloon and you think it won't pop? Of course it will.

A: No! It won't.

B: OK. Go ahead.

[Bobby puts his fingers in his ears as Amber brings the pointed end of the needle to the balloon.]

A: Now watch.

B: I'm watching, I'm watching. Hurry and do it. I don't like loud pops.

[Amber pushes the needle into the balloon.]

Wow. How can that be happening? The balloon didn't pop.

A: Keep watching now.

[Amber continues pushing the needle through the balloon. Then she pushes it through and out the other side.]

Figure 3-6

B: Gee whiz, Amber! How'd you do that? Let me see it.

A: Sure. Here, take my balloon (Figure 3–6).

B: That's really amazing.

A: Do you want to push one through?

B: Yes, yes. Let me try it.

A: Here's another needle. Go ahead. But you might not be able to do it like I can.

B: If you can do it, then I can. Here goes.

[Bobby pushes the needle into the balloon and it bursts with a loud "POP."]

A: Too bad.

B: OK, Amber. Tell me how you did that.

A: It's just magic.

⊙ Description

What You Need

1. Several medium-sized round balloons
2. Two thin steel (not aluminum!) knitting needles or two thin steel rods from a hardware store (they should be long enough to go through the balloon when it is inflated)
3. A fine metal file
4. A lubricant such as vegetable or mineral oil, or better yet, WD-40

How to Do It

File the pointed ends of both knitting needles or rods to very sharp points with the metal file. Be very careful with the needles after you do this because they are dangerous. Inflate two or more of the balloons so that they are a little less than fully inflated. Tie them off.

Hold the balloon carefully on a table as shown in Figure 3–7. At the very bottom of the balloon exactly opposite from where you tied it off, there is a small circle of color that is slightly less transparent than the sides of the balloon. Push the point of the needle right into the center of this spot. (It helps if you cover the needle with a little vegetable or mineral oil or WD-40, and rotate it a bit back and forth as you push it in.)

Continue pushing the needle into the balloon until the pointed tip is near the opposite end, *right next to the knot you tied.* Now push the needle through the balloon at this point, and slide down the needle so it is centered as previously shown in Figure 3–6.

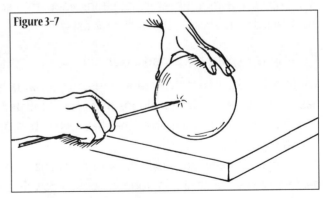

Figure 3–7

Ask your observer if he or she wants to try it, and hand them another sharp knitting needle. Hold your balloon with the needle through it near them. Make sure they do not push their needle through right next to yours, because there's a chance that it might work. Most people will not. Regardless of where else they push the needle in, the balloon will burst.

How It Works

The balloon doesn't burst when you push the needle through because you penetrate the only two places where the rubber of the balloon is thick and strong enough not to be torn open by the pressure of the gas inside. When you blow up a balloon, the rubber stretches and gets thinner and thinner as more and more air is blown inside. However, at the very bottom and top of the balloon, this stretching is much less than everywhere else, so the rubber is still relatively thick and strong at these points.

When the needle punctures the thicker rubber at the bottom and top, the pressure of the air inside the balloon is not sufficient to continue expanding the hole into a large tear. Instead, this relatively thick rubber seals itself around the needle as it enters the balloon and the air cannot escape. The same thing happens as the needle exits through the thick rubber near the knot.

When your observer pushes the needle into the side or any other area of the balloon where the rubber is thinner, a small hole is made in this thin surface. Because the rubber is so thin, the tiny hole rapidly develops into a large tear as gas pressure inside the balloon rips it open. The thin rubber is not strong enough to seal itself around the needle and keep the air inside. As a result, the balloon bursts.

Variations, Explorations, and Extensions

Try to penetrate two different balloons on the same knitting needle. To do this you will need a very long needle or balloons that are not inflated too much so they are small enough to fit on a regular knitting needle. The effect of two balloons on the needle is even more impressive than just one.

You can penetrate a balloon with other sharp items besides knitting needles. A local hardware store will have thin, round, wooden dowels and rods that work just as well. Shishkebob sticks from the grocery store will also work if you sand them very smooth.

You might try different kinds and shapes of balloons to see which work best and which don't work at all. Can you push a needle through a long balloon, end to end? Of course, the effect is much more easily detected in a long balloon. Since you must go end to end, this will be obvious to an observer. It is much less obvious with a round balloon, which is much more symmetrical. Will the effect work if you fill the balloon with water instead of air? Why or why not? Try it (over the sink) and see.

How long will a balloon on a needle stay inflated compared to a regular tied-off balloon that doesn't have a needle through it? Is air leaking where the needle penetrates the balloon? Try pulling the needle out of the balloon. How rapidly does it deflate? Can you blow the balloon up again? Why or why not?

On an uninflated round balloon draw a quarter-inch line on the very bottom, opposite the open end, using a ballpoint pen. Make a similar quarter-inch line on the side of the uninflated balloon. Blow up the balloon and tie it off with a knot. Now measure the two lines you just made. Write down the length of each.

If you divide the length of the bottom line on the inflated balloon (measured in inches) by the original length of this line on the uninflated balloon, you will see how much the rubber has stretched at the bottom. If you do the same thing for the line on the side, you will see how much the rubber has stretched at the side. Now you can compare the amount of stretching at the bottom with the amount of stretching on the side. Which is greater? Why?

◎ What You See and What You Don't

What a casual observer doesn't notice in this effect is that the place where the needle is inserted into the balloon, and also where it exits, are very carefully selected. The experience most people have had with balloons is that they always burst when punctured by a sharp object. With a round balloon there is an assumption that all places on the surface are the same, except perhaps where the knot is. And no one thinks that area of the balloon is particularly special.

The thickness of the rubber in a balloon is so small that our eyes cannot detect the difference between, say, .008 inches (the sides) and .004 inches (the bottom). But of course that's doubling the thickness, which can make a substantial difference in the stretching and tearing properties of the rubber. For our eyes, doubling something very small still results in something very small. Without a measuring device called a *micrometer*, we can't really detect the difference at all. However, this small difference is sufficient to allow the balloon to stay together if penetrated at the bottom and top, whereas it bursts if penetrated from the side.

A careful observer will note, especially if you do this more than once, that you have selectively penetrated only the top and bottom of the balloon. This is particularly apparent if you put two balloons on one needle. So when you put just one on and ask the observer if he or she would like to try it, you accomplish two things at once.

First, the observer will push the needle through somewhere away from yours. The balloon will burst. That shows you can do it and they can't. Second, the balloon is no longer available for examination, so it's not obvious that it needed to be penetrated at specific locations on the surface. You must not do this illusion more than once! A good observer will be able to see you carefully selecting the correct places to penetrate the balloon the second time. The first time you do it, the observer's attention is not focused on this detail. Observers are anticipating the bursting balloon and may even have their fingers in their ears. The second time, this isn't the case. Their interest and attention are more carefully focused on exactly what you are doing, and they may well see that the top and bottom of the balloon have been carefully selected.

◎ A Deeper Look

Figure 3–8 is a diagram of an inflated, round balloon, tied off with a knot. The arrows in the balloon pointing toward the inside surface represent the pressure of the gas in the balloon. This gas is a mixture of oxygen, nitrogen, and carbon dioxide molecules, all of which are moving very fast and colliding with the inside surface. These collisions cause the pressure exerted by the gas inside the balloon, which keeps it inflated against the slightly lower *atmospheric pressure* outside the balloon (represented by the arrows outside).

The atmospheric pressure results from the weight of air in the atmosphere. The pressure inside a balloon must be greater than the atmospheric pressure in order to stretch the rubber and keep the balloon inflated.

Figure 3–9 shows a thick region of the balloon wall, at the end opposite the knot, being penetrated by a needle. This is compared to a thin region at the side of the balloon being penetrated by a needle. In the thick region, there is enough rubber to hold the balloon together.

As the main body of the needle expands into the initial hole, the thick rubber expands around it, forming an expanding seal as the needle penetrates.

In the thin region, the needle starts a small hole and there isn't enough rubber to seal the balloon tightly to the needle. The air inside the balloon pushes against the small hole right where the needle enters. Because the rubber is so thin, the gas begins to escape and it tears a larger hole as it does. This larger hole rapidly expands as the thin rubber tears, and all the gas escapes as the balloon bursts.

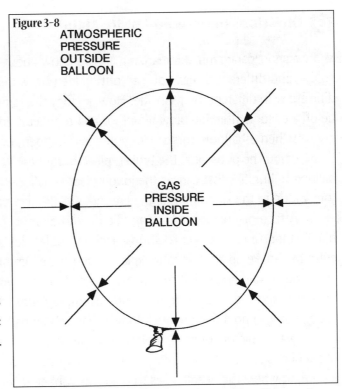

Figure 3-8

ATMOSPHERIC PRESSURE OUTSIDE BALLOON

GAS PRESSURE INSIDE BALLOON

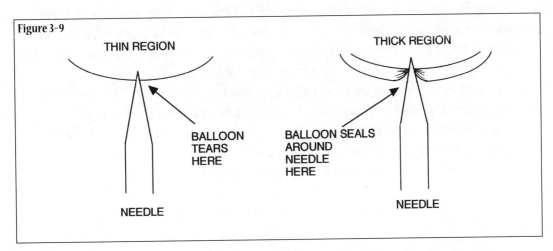

Figure 3-9

THIN REGION

THICK REGION

BALLOON TEARS HERE

BALLOON SEALS AROUND NEEDLE HERE

NEEDLE

NEEDLE

⊙ Questions to Draw and Write About

Write a short paragraph summarizing all you know about balloons. Consider sizes, shapes, colors, and different things you can put inside (air, water, helium). How are the balloons different with different things inside? How are they the same? What happens when you don't tie off a balloon after you blow air into it and then let it go? Why does it move like it does?

When a balloon bursts, can you see it happen, or do you just see the balloon and then— after the pop—just the broken piece of rubber? What are the ways you can cause a balloon to burst? What causes the loud noise? A balloon filled with water bursts when you throw it up in the air and it hits the ground. An air-filled balloon doesn't. Why?

After a day or two, a balloon filled with helium begins to get smaller. It takes an air-filled balloon much longer to shrink. Helium molecules are much smaller than the molecules that make up air. Can you explain why the helium balloon shrinks more rapidly? As a clue, you should know that the rubber of a balloon has very tiny holes all over it. This may help you explain the behavior of air and helium. Mylar balloons (the shiny ones that look like aluminum foil) hold helium much longer than rubber balloons. Why might this be so?

Draw a picture of small molecules of air or helium escaping through the porous sides of a rubber balloon. Draw a picture of the penetrated balloon. Magnify the portion of the balloon right where the needle goes through the rubber at the bottom.

Imagine you are very small and sitting right at the end of the needle as it is pushed through the balloon (so it doesn't burst). Describe what you see and feel. What is it like as you go from the outside to the inside of the balloon? Describe what you see and feel when the needle is pushed into the side of the balloon and it bursts.

Pretend you are a molecule of air inside an inflated, tied-off balloon. Write a description of what it feels like when a needle is pushed into the side of the balloon and it bursts. Consider your situation before and after the balloon bursts. How is it different before and after?

Draw a cartoon of a balloon being punctured by a needle. Make up a funny caption for the cartoon in which the balloon says something. You might put a face on the balloon in your cartoon.

Magical Movements

Solids, Liquids, Gases, Mass, and Density

CHAPTER

4

 Rising and Falling: Dissolved Gases

 **Dialogue**

Paige: I can make things rise up and then fall. And then rise and fall, over and over
without even touching them.

Bobby: No, you can't.

P: I can too.

B: OK. Make my bike rise up in the air and then fall down.

P: I can't do it with your bike, but I can with fruit.

B: Fruit?! OK, here's a banana. Raise it to the ceiling without touching it.

P: I'm going to use cherries and I'm not going to make them rise up in the air. I'm
going to do it in a glass of soda.

B: In soda? I don't think you can do it there either.

P: I can too. Watch.

[Paige fills a large glass with sparkling water and puts in three large, red cherries.]

B: They're just sitting there in the bottom of the glass.

P: Wait a minute, please. You're very impatient, Bobby.

B: I am not. You said you could make them rise and they're just . . .

[A cherry floats to the top of the glass of soda and then starts to sink.]

P: See!

B: Hey, how did that happen?

[Another cherry rises and sinks.]

P: I told you I could do it. All of the cherries are now rising and falling.

B: Why are they doing that? Why don't they stay at the top or bottom? They should just float like a cork, or sink like a rock. I've never seen anything float and sink and float and. . . . What's happening?

P: Magic!

B: It is not.

P: Is too.

B: Not!

P: Is.

◉ Description

What You Need

1. A tall glass

2. A bottle of sparkling water or other clear carbonated beverage

3. Some ripe red cherries.

How to Do It

Pour the carbonated water or soda into a tall glass. Add three of the ripe red cherries. They will quickly sink to the bottom of the glass. But wait for half a minute and you will be surprised to see that they magically float to the surface and then sink again to the bottom. In a few more seconds, they will rise again to the top and then sink again. This rising and falling will continue for some time. Those cherries look alive, don't they? How can that be? What makes them move?

How It Works

If you look carefully at your glass of sparkling water you will notice small bubbles rising to the surface all the time. They rise because the gas inside the bubbles is much lighter than the liquid. The bubbles form from carbon dioxide, which is dissolved in the soda. They don't form until you take the cap off the soda and release the pressure. When bubbles form in soda they quickly rise to the surface and burst at the top, releasing the carbon dioxide gas into the air.

When you add cherries to soda, they sink to the bottom of the glass because they are just a bit heavier than the liquid. However, after a few moments, bubbles of carbon dioxide gas form and stick to their skin. When enough bubbles of gas stick, they lift the cherry from the bottom of the glass to the top. When the cherry reaches the top of the glass, the bubbles on the cherry skin burst and release the gas into the air. The cherry without the attached bubbles is now heavier than the liquid, and it sinks to the bottom again. The whole process is then repeated. When all the carbon dioxide gas is released from the soda, the cherries will stay at the bottom, but this takes quite some time.

Variations, Explorations, and Extensions

Try some different fruits and vegetables. Raisins, grapes, chopped up bits of carrot or apple, peas, and corn kernels are a few things you might try. Would a strawberry work? Why or why not? Try one and see. How about lead fishing weights? Why don't they work? You could also try different kinds of liquids. Which works best, ginger ale, club soda, or 7-UP? Does diet 7-UP work better than regular 7-UP? Experiment and see!

You can make your own liquid containing carbon dioxide bubbles from vinegar and baking soda. Fill a very large glass about one-third full of vinegar. Add several large tablespoons of baking soda. After the initial large release of gaseous carbon dioxide, the remaining liquid will have bubbles of carbon dioxide rising up, just like soda. You can use this liquid to raise and lower cherries or other items.

Put an unopened can of diet soda and an unopened can of regular soda in a large bucket of water or in a bathtub filled with water. The regular soda will sink, but the diet soda won't. Why do you think this happens?

◉ What You See and What You Don't

When cherries are rising and falling in a glass of soda, what you notice most are the cherries themselves. And you direct the observer's attention toward them, not toward the bubbles. Of course, you also see the bubbles on each cherry as it rises to the surface, but these are fairly small. When the bubbles burst after reaching the surface, you don't notice at all that the number of bubbles on the surface of the cherry drops significantly. This is because the bubbles are too small and the cherries are moving. It's impossible to count tiny bubbles on a moving cherry.

Figure 4-1

If you look carefully at a cherry that has just sunk from the top, you will notice that there are far fewer bubbles on its surface than on a cherry just beginning to rise up (Figure 4–1). New bubbles are forming on the surface of cherries at the bottom at the same time that old ones are bursting on the surface of cherries at the top. And bubbles are rising all through the soda. Because of this, attention is not focused at all toward bubbles on the surface of any individual cherry.

Cherries almost float in water all by themselves. When you do this magical effect, make sure you don't use that odd cherry with a hollow inside or some other structural feature that makes it float by itself.

◉ A Deeper Look

Carbon dioxide is a colorless gas that is much more soluble in water than the main gaseous components of air, nitrogen and oxygen. The formula for a carbon dioxide molecule is CO_2. This means that one carbon dioxide molecule is composed of one carbon atom, C, and two oxygen atoms, O. To make a carbonated beverage, carbon dioxide is bubbled into water (or a water solution that also contains flavoring and sugar) at double the atmospheric pressure. The solubility of carbon dioxide in the liquid at this high pressure is much greater than at normal atmospheric pressure, so it dissolves in the liquid to a much greater extent.

This whole process of dissolving carbon dioxide in water under high pressure is called *carbonation*. If the liquid with dissolved carbon dioxide gas at high pressure is sealed in a can or bottle, the gas will stay dissolved in the liquid. The high pressure of carbon dioxide gas above the liquid in a sealed bottle or can keeps the dissolved gas from coming out. However, when the cap is removed you hear a pop, which is the rush of high-pressure carbon dioxide gas above the liquid escaping from the container. As soon as this occurs, the dissolved gas in the liquid begins to come out by forming bubbles throughout the liquid. These bubbles are mostly carbon dioxide, but they contain a small amount of water vapor. Because carbon dioxide gas is much lighter than the liquid, it rises to the surface as bubbles that burst, releasing the gas into the atmosphere.

Any object dropped into a carbonated beverage will have a surface upon which small bubbles of carbon dioxide gas can grow. This happens because of small surface irregularities that act as sites where bubble formation is favored (where carbon dioxide molecules can collect). The bubbles are weakly bonded to the surface of the object because of an electrostatic force.

If the object is very heavy, like an iron nail, the bubbles that form on the surface will get bigger and bigger until their buoyancy increases enough so that they break away from the nail and rise to the surface. If the object is only slightly heavier than water (such as a cherry), and if a sufficient number of small bubbles form on it before they break away and float to the surface, then their combined buoyancy can lift the object up to the surface. This is what happens when the cherry rises to the surface of the soda.

As soon as the object comes to the surface, the bubbles burst. When a sufficient number of bubbles on the surface of the object have burst, then the object sinks to the bottom again. The process repeats itself, and will continue to do so until there is no more dissolved carbon dioxide gas in the liquid.

Sometimes heavy objects that have sunk in the ocean can be brought to the surface in the same way a cherry is brought to the surface of a glass of soda. Large inflatable balloons can be tightly attached to or inserted into the object and then inflated with air, which raises the object to the surface. If the object has hollow sections inside, air can be pumped directly into them to raise it.

In this discussion we have talked about the *weight* of a cherry. More correctly, we should talk about the *density* of a cherry. The density of any substance is the weight of a specific volume of it. For example, the weight of one cubic centimeter of water is about one gram. The density of water is therefore about one gram per cubic centimeter.

The weight of a sinking cherry that might have a volume of one cubic centimeter will be a bit greater than one gram. The density of such a cherry is greater than the density of water. Objects that have densities greater than one gram per cubic centimeter (nails, rocks, bricks, etc.) all sink in water, regardless of their volume. Objects that have densities less than one gram per cubic centimeter (cork, most wood, ice, etc.) will float in water, regardless of their size (Figure 4-2). Floating objects displace (push into) a volume of water equal to their weight. The rest of the object sticks out above the surface.

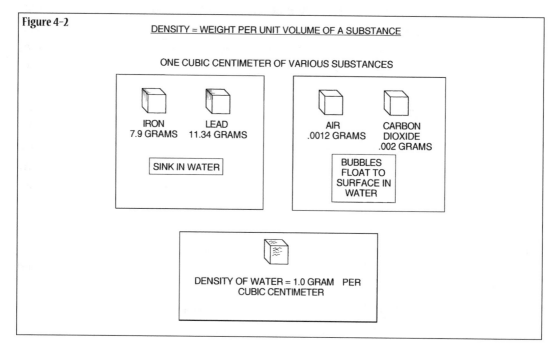

Figure 4-2

DENSITY = WEIGHT PER UNIT VOLUME OF A SUBSTANCE

ONE CUBIC CENTIMETER OF VARIOUS SUBSTANCES

IRON
7.9 GRAMS

LEAD
11.34 GRAMS

AIR
.0012 GRAMS

CARBON
DIOXIDE
.002 GRAMS

SINK IN WATER

BUBBLES
FLOAT TO
SURFACE IN
WATER

DENSITY OF WATER = 1.0 GRAM PER
CUBIC CENTIMETER

Questions to Draw and Write About

Draw what you see when you drop a cherry into a glass of soda. Why do the bubbles on a cherry break when the cherry floats up to the surface of the soda?

Why will some fruits and vegetables be brought to the surface of a glass of soda by bubbles sticking to them, while others won't? If you tied a whole bunch of cherries together with a thread and put them in a glass of water, would they rise to the surface? Why or why not? Can you do an experiment to find out?

Make a list of objects that you know float in water and a list of objects that you know sink. Corks float and thumbtacks sink. Do you think that you could push enough thumbtacks into a small cork to make it sink? Does it make a difference how big the cork is? Can a cork with thumbtacks in it be made to rise and sink in soda like a cherry? Design some experiments to find out the answers to these questions.

Imagine you are very tiny and sitting on a cherry that has just been dropped into a glass of soda. Get a tight grip and describe what you see and experience as the cherry sinks to the bottom of the glass, is slowly covered with bubbles, and then rises to the surface. What do you see around you? Do you enjoy the ride? What is the liquid like? Are any bubbles forming on you?

Draw a cartoon strip with animated cherries talking about falling and rising in a glass of soda. Have them comment to each other about what is happening and how they are feeling.

Surprising Spoon: Breaking Bonds

Dialogue

José: I can bend this spoon completely in half with my mind. All I have to do is concentrate very hard.

Paige: Oh sure, José. And I can flap my arms and fly.

J: No, I really can do it.

[José first holds the spoon up by the handle. He bangs the oval end down on the table several times, showing the spoon to be quite solid.]

P: You'll bend it completely in half?

J: Yes. Now watch.

[Taking the spoon very carefully, José places it between the thumb and index finger of his right hand, arranging it vertically. Holding the spoon in front of his face, and using only the fingers of his right hand, he shakes it gently back and forth. His brow is furrowed as he looks very hard at the spoon, concentrating on it. (See Figure 4–3.)]

I have to concentrate really hard to do this. It takes a lot of mental energy, you know. Sometimes I don't have enough.

P: You're just shaking it. You aren't bending it.

J: Keep watching.

P: Nothing's happening. You're just moving it around. You can't . . .

[Slowly the oval part of the spoon starts to bend sideways as José continues to gently move the whole spoon back and forth.]

What?! How are you doing that?

J: I'm concentrating very hard Paige, I told you.

[The spoon continues to bend, seemingly by itself, as José holds it up in his fingers.]

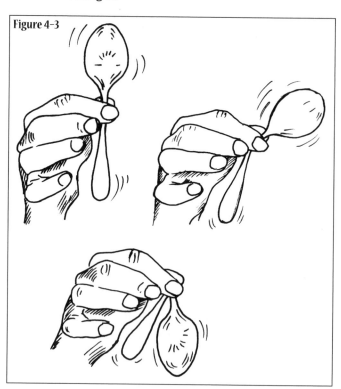

Figure 4-3

He continues to focus his eyes on it, slowly shaking it back and forth. It continues to bend further and further over until the oval part is at right angles to the handle.]

P: I really can't believe you're really doing that.

J: How else could it be happening, Paige?

[The oval part now bends around toward the handle as oval and handle almost touch. Paige is amazed.]

P: I don't see how this can be happening.

J: I've got incredible mental powers, Paige. You may not believe it, but it's true.

P: You do not.

J: I do too.

[José drops the completely bent spoon on the table. It hits the table top as two pieces. The handle is completely separated from the oval. Paige picks them up.]

P: OK, José. Tell me how you did that.

J: Incredible mental powers.

P: Stop saying that. It isn't true.

J: It is.

P: No, it isn't.

J: Then you tell me how I did it.

P: I don't know. It just happened!

[Paige picks up the two pieces of spoon and examines them with a puzzled look.]

◉ Description

What You Need

1. Several expendable metal teaspoons (not part of an expensive set of utensils). The best kind are narrow where the oval meets the handle. Spoons with horizontal designs imprinted in the metal work best, but any teaspoon will work. These can be purchased at a grocery, hardware, or discount store.

2. A large, heavy-duty pair of pliers

How to Do It

Have your parents or teacher help you prepare the spoon. Grab the spoon handle very tightly with the pliers right below the oval of the spoon. With your other hand, bend the spoon very quickly perpendicular to the handle. As soon as you have done this, bend it back straight again. Then bend it back perpendicular to the handle. Continue to do this back and forth, bending until you feel it is getting easier. The metal at the point where the spoon handle is being bent will become quite hot (in fact, hot enough to burn you, so don't touch it).

Now here's the tricky part. If you keep on bending the spoon back and forth, it will eventually break at the point of the bend. What you want to do is bend it back and forth sufficiently to cause it to just *begin* to break, but to stop right before it breaks completely. And you want to stop with the spoon in the straight, not bent, position. This may be a bit difficult to do the first time you try. Get a few extra spoons so you can do it several times if you don't get it right.

If you do it just right, the final straight spoon will have a hairline crack in it, right where you have been bending it. There is only a small bit of metal holding the oval and handle together, but when the spoon cools back to room temperature, it is enough so that you can handle the spoon as if it were normal. You can even bang it gently on the table and it won't break, but wait till you carry out the illusion in front of an observer before you do this. It will make the illusion all the more astounding. The hairline crack is not detectable unless you are looking for it. Do NOT let the observer examine or handle the spoon.

After preparing the spoon, you may put it away. When you are ready to do the illusion you should begin by talking about your mental powers, the force of your mind, how you can make objects move, and other gibberish. But be serious about it! You are acting here, and your act will determine how well the illusion works. If you don't lie really well, the illusion works much less effectively.

Bang the spoon gently on the table to show it is solid, then quickly grab the oval of the spoon in your left hand. Grab the handle between the thumb and index finger of your right hand, *right over the hairline crack.* The rest of the fingers of your right hand should grab the spoon tightly around the handle. Pretend to carefully position the spoon. Apply a very slight but sideways force (in a direction perpendicular to the original bending motion). This motion is very slight and will not be detected by observers, but it is sufficient to crack the spoon in half. Make sure to keep the oval and handle straight, as if they were still connected. Now hold them together using only the thumb and index finger of your right hand.

By holding the spoon at an angle and lessening the pressure of your fingers over the hairline crack, you can slowly allow the broken-off oval part of the spoon to fall to the side (make sure you do not let it drop completely yet). You can practice this with a completely broken spoon. To your audience, the spoon is still whole, and it appears as if the oval is bending from the handle. Actually, it is broken and you are hiding the break between your thumb and index finger, which also hold the two pieces together. Gravity is doing the "bending" here. The more you let the oval drop to the side by releasing and applying pressure with your thumb and index finger, the larger the "bend" appears to get. By moving the spoon around you can get the oval to "bend" all the way back toward the handle while you make a pretense of straining and concentrating very hard to achieve this amazing feat.

When the spoon is finally "bent" to a maximum, you can release it and let the two pieces fall to the table. If you're really good at pretending, you can appear exhausted from all your mental effort. Then you might say something like, "Though I can accomplish this, I really don't have any idea of how I do it or what makes it happen."

How It Works

Metals have a unique kind of atomic structure that allows them to be bent and dented. You can't bend a crystal of quartz, a piece of glass, or a chunk of granite. When you bend a narrow piece of metal repeatedly, it gets hotter and hotter. Bending motions alternately break and re-form the bonds that hold the atoms in the metal next to each other. The forces that hold the metal together are reduced from the bending motion, making it easier for you to break the metal. When enough of them do this, the metal will come apart.

This is exactly what is happening in the spoon handle when you bend it back and forth to prepare it for this illusion. If you stop bending before all the metal atom bonds are broken, the few remaining bonds will hold the metal together. The spoon appears whole. But of course it isn't whole at all. There are fewer metal atoms bonded together than in an uncracked spoon. These hold the spoon in its regular shape as a single piece of metal.

This is the tricky part. The last few metal atom bonds in the remaining bit of metal that isn't cracked are easily broken by a much smaller force than you'd need to break the original uncracked spoon. Holding the pieces together between your thumb and index finger, you apply this force, but you do it in a way that hides the final breaking process. You keep the broken pieces together and aligned so that the spoon looks whole and unbroken. *You mustn't let the observer detect the motion that breaks the spoon in half.*

Holding the two broken pieces between your thumb and index finger as if they were whole allows you to use the force of gravity to slowly "bend" the spoon. You must use the pressure of your fingers very carefully here, relaxing them just enough to let the oval fall a bit to the side very slowly, but not so much that you drop the pieces. After you squeeze them together to stop it from falling, then relax them a bit again to let the oval drop further. This will take some practice. You can lengthen the whole process for a minute or two as you strain to use all your "mental powers." Pass the time by talking about your psychokinetic brain vibrations, neuronal quantum waves, or other interesting things you think up.

Variations, Explorations, and Extensions

This effect works just as well with a fork as with a spoon. You will need to examine a variety of spoons and forks to see which ones work best. Some utensils have very thick handles that are difficult to crack, even with a pair of pliers.

If you have trouble cracking the spoon and it seems to break before you stop bending it, you can try joining the pieces together with some extra-strength glue. However, the glue must hold sufficiently well so that you can handle the spoon as if it were not broken. You can also experiment and use a very small bit of silver paint to cover any cracks that appear too large.

You will need practice to make this illusion perfect. After a few trial runs using a broken spoon, you will get the knack of how to hold the broken pieces together and release the pressure with your fingers to let them slowly fall apart ("bend"). You should slowly shake your hand back and forth as you let them fall. This hides the straight falling motion by adding a motion you are in control of, making it look as if the shaking is, in part, accomplishing the task of bending (which of course makes no sense at all to an observer and further hides what is really going on). In addition, the shaking helps loosen the metal in your fingers, allowing it to move without your releasing it.

You needn't break a spoon each time to practice letting the broken pieces of the spoon slowly fall. However, cracking and breaking the spoon with a short sideways force does require a partially cracked spoon each time you do it. Try to find some inexpensive spoons at a grocery store or garage sale.

Experiment with different kinds of metals. Go to a hardware store and purchase some small pieces of heavy copper wire and aluminum wire (not the multi-stranded type, but single, large heavy strands—the kind used for electrical wiring in homes). Compare these in terms of how much each must be bent back and forth before it breaks. Which is easiest to break? Do the wires become hot before they break? What do you notice about the region of wire that has been bent back and forth repeatedly? Is it different in any way from that part of the wire that wasn't bent (in color or texture)? If there is a difference, what do you think might cause it?

Metals conduct heat quite differently than other kinds of solids. Take a long piece of white chalk (made of the compound calcium carbonate) and a small piece of metal about the same size (a small piece of pipe from the hardware store). Hold the chalk in the hot portion of a candle flame for a while. Does the chalk get hot where you are holding it with your hand? Do the same thing with the piece of metal. Does the metal get hot where you are holding it with your hand? Be careful. Don't burn yourself.

Metals conduct electricity quite differently than other kinds of solids. To conduct electricity a substance must have electrons that can freely move. Take a flashlight battery and two copper wires. Using tape, connect one wire to the battery's positive end and the other to the negative end. Take the opposite ends of the wires and complete a circuit to a flashlight bulb so that it lights up. Now put different kinds of solids into the circuit. Get help from your teacher or a parent if you need to. Try different metals (iron, copper, aluminum) and different nonmetals (plastic, wood, glass). What do you notice? Why do you think metals are different from nonmetals? Go to the Deeper Look section of Surprising Spoon and read about the atomic structure of metals.

Examine the dialogue between José and Paige. Do you think José does a good job of misleading Paige? If not, can you construct a better dialogue? What kinds of things might you say to mislead an observer of this illusion? Could you use a magnet and pretend to pull the top of the spoon over to the side? How would the dialogue change if you did this?

Why won't this illusion work if you try to do it a second time? What would observers ask you if you tried doing it over again? Would their behavior be different when they were seeing it the second time? In what way? What would they immediately want to see when you pulled out a second spoon? What parts of this illusion do you find the hardest to do? Why?

◉ What You See and What You Don't

This illusion is the same as that used by a well-known psychic from the Middle East to demonstrate his "mental powers." When done properly—with good acting, an appropriate script, and a presentation that seems spontaneously genuine—it is astoundingly effective. If you do it right, nothing can be detected. When the illusion is over, observers can examine the pieces very carefully.

The illusion depends very much on:

1. preparing the spoon properly;
2. convincing your audience it is a normal spoon by holding the handle and banging it (very gently) on a table;
3. breaking the spoon completely once the crack is hidden between your fingers without your audience being aware this is done;
4. keeping the two pieces together between your thumb and index finger so the spoon looks whole and unbroken;
5. a gentle shaking movement of the seemingly connected pieces, during which the oval part of the spoon is allowed to slowly drop to the side and down;
6. using effective dialogue and a presentation that appears genuine;
7. practicing a number of times before you do it.

A number of things are hidden in this illusion, and there is much misdirection and misleading language. The crack in the prepared spoon is completely hidden because it is too small to see if you aren't looking for it. The illusion can never be done more than once, for your audience will want to inspect the spoon more carefully before you begin the second time. And they will be sure to spot the crack. The first time you do it, they really don't know what to expect or look for. Banging this seemingly whole spoon on the table while holding it by the handle is very convincing evidence that it is indeed whole, even though it is cracked almost through.

Once the crack is hidden between the fingers, the movement that breaks the two pieces apart occurs without the audience being aware it has happened. Since only a very small movement is needed, this is easily accomplished by moving the whole spoon a bit as the break is completed. Appropriate descriptive lying can be added if you wish. With conviction and feeling, announce, "I am aligning the spoon with the force field coming from the psychokinetic lobe of my brain," or some other nonsense, as you make the slight adjustment that cracks the pieces apart. No one could break a normal spoon in half without much more effort than your audience will see you use. Once the spoon is completely "bent" around on itself, the separate pieces can then be dropped on the table for all to examine. The effect is astonishing.

The primary key in this illusion is the observers' belief that the spoon is whole in the beginning. You have convinced them of this by banging the spoon on the table and showing it to them—whole! No one will imagine a tiny bit of metal left in a cracked spoon could keep it looking whole.

After the spoon is broken, the slow movement of the pieces from a straight alignment at zero degrees to a ninety-degree angle and, eventually, to a completely bent one-hundred-and-eighty-degree angle is interpreted by observers as a bending of the metal rather than as a reorientation of two separate pieces. This is particularly so if it happens very slowly. The illusion of the spoon bending is almost absolute since there is no other way an unbroken spoon could do this. If you believe the spoon is whole, which is what you saw, what else could be happening? Since no visible force seems applied as the spoon "bends"—the actual force causing the movement is simply gravity—nonsense explanations about mental powers might seem the only acceptable alternative for an unsuspecting and gullible observer. This illusion is the biggest lie in this book! The illusion Amazing Quarter is the second biggest.

Everyone will demand to know how it works. You must not tell them! Otherwise you become a simple liar. What a letdown that would be. Keep up the psychokinetic brain wave mumbo jumbo. Eventually you give in and say "Well, OK. It works the same way as this amazing string," which you just happen to have in your pocket. Then go into the Amazing String illusion, using dialogue about fusion forces, fibrous joining fields, etc.

◉ A Deeper Look

There are all kinds of solids that exist in the world, such as rocks, bricks, salt, glass, diamonds, gold, and iron. Rocks, bricks, salt, and glass are complex chemical compounds composed of several different elements in specific proportions. Diamonds, gold, and iron are each single elements. There are a variety of different types of solids, and they can be categorized based on their atomic structure as noted below:

> *Ionic Solids,* such as table salt (sodium chloride, which is NaCl), are composed of positive and negative particles called ions (sodium ion Na^+, which is positive and chloride ion Cl^-, which is negative). Ionic solids have no discrete molecules. Molecules are small collections of atoms in fixed ratios, and are described below under the category of covalent solids.

> *Metallic Solids,* such as iron, silver, and copper, are composed of metal atoms (or positive metal ions, M^+, floating in a sea of negative electrons, e^-).

> *Covalent Solids,* such as water (H_2O), carbon dioxide (CO_2), and oxygen (O_2), exist as molecules held together by bonds in which the atoms share their electrons. Molecules in such solids are attracted to each other by weak electrical forces.

There are other kinds of solids as well, including network solids (diamond is an example) and amorphous solids (glass is an example). Metals have different properties from either ionic or covalent solids. They conduct electricity. They are also ductile and can be made into wires. They are malleable and can be rolled into sheets.

The ductility and malleability of metal are particularly important in the illusion Surprising Spoon. These properties result from the unique atomic structure of solid metal, which is quite different from that of either ionic or covalent solids. You can't make salt or ice into a wire or roll them into sheets. Instead, they crack into pieces. Structures of the ionic solid sodium chloride (table salt), the covalent solid ice (solid water), and the metallic solid iron are shown in Figure 4–4.

The ionic solid has very strong bonds (attractive forces) between the sodium and chloride ions, which results in a very rigid cubic structure. When strong force is applied to a crystal of salt, it shatters into smaller cubic units. When strong force is applied to a crystal of ice, it also shatters into smaller pieces. The structure of a metal, however, with positive ions floating in a sea of electrons, allows the metal to be distorted considerably before it breaks or shatters. It is not as rigid as salt or water, even though the bonds from particle to particle are very strong. A chunk of metal can be stretched and distorted but still remain a single piece.

When solids are heated, their constituent parts (atoms or molecules) begin to vibrate more rapidly. The higher the temperature, the more they vibrate. At a very high temperature—the melting point—they vibrate so rapidly that the structure of the solid breaks down and a liquid forms. In a liquid, the atoms or ions move around easily. A liquid has no definite shape, but takes the shape of its container. Covalent solids melt at a relatively low temperature. For example, ice melts at zero degrees centigrade. Both ionic and metallic solids melt at much

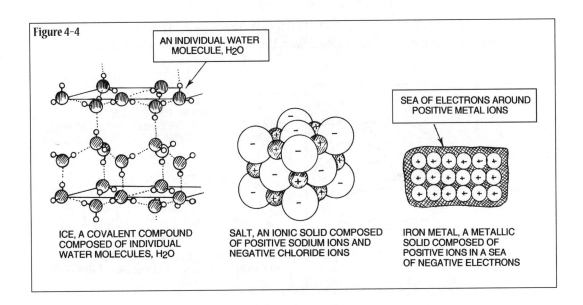

Figure 4-4

AN INDIVIDUAL WATER MOLECULE, H_2O

SEA OF ELECTRONS AROUND POSITIVE METAL IONS

ICE, A COVALENT COMPOUND COMPOSED OF INDIVIDUAL WATER MOLECULES, H_2O

SALT, AN IONIC SOLID COMPOSED OF POSITIVE SODIUM IONS AND NEGATIVE CHLORIDE IONS

IRON METAL, A METALLIC SOLID COMPOSED OF POSITIVE IONS IN A SEA OF NEGATIVE ELECTRONS higher temperatures. At very high temperatures that are still below their melting point, metals may become more ductile and malleable than at lower temperatures.

As you prepare the spoon for Surprising Spoon by bending it back and forth a number of times, the metal ions in the spoon move back and forth out of their stable arrangements. As the back-and-forth bending force continues to be applied, the particles move more, to the point where the metal structure is distorted (at the bend). The temperature of the metal at this point will increase rapidly and particle motion at the atomic level increases. When the motion of the particles (and the temperature of the metal) gets sufficiently large, the bonds between particles responsible for the structure of the metal will break. At this point, the metal will crack. This is exactly what occurs at the point where the oval of the spoon and handle are being bent back and forth (Figure 4–5). If the bending motion is stopped quickly, the temperature of the metal at the bend will rapidly drop back down. If a small part of the metal has not yet cracked at this point, it may be sufficiently strong when cooled to hold the metal together even though most of the rest of the metal is cracked through (Figure 4–6).

If the spoon is brought back to its original shape, the crack will not be readily apparent. The number of particles in the cracked region that have separated is very small compared to the rest of the metal in the spoon handle, which remains unbroken. And if the small region of uncracked metal holds the spoon together, then it appears just as it did before it was cracked— as long as the bending motion was stopped with the spoon in the straight position.

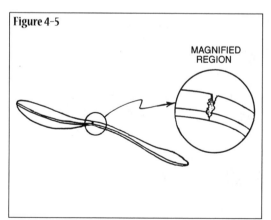

Figure 4-5

MAGNIFIED REGION

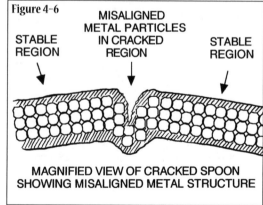

Figure 4-6

STABLE REGION

MISALIGNED METAL PARTICLES IN CRACKED REGION

STABLE REGION

MAGNIFIED VIEW OF CRACKED SPOON SHOWING MISALIGNED METAL STRUCTURE

⊙ Questions to Draw and Write About

Using a magnifying glass or a 3-D binocular microscope, examine very carefully the crack in a spoon prepared for the illusion. Draw an accurate picture of this region of the handle. Looking at the depth of the crack from the edge of the spoon, how much of the metal is cracked and how much is still intact? Examine several spoons that you have prepared for this illusion and compare them. Are the cracks all about the same depth or do they vary a great deal?

The electrical and heat-conducting properties of metals are closely related to those properties that allow a metal spoon to be bent back and forth and increase in temperature. Can you describe and draw pictures to explain what is happening on an atomic scale when a spoon begins to crack? Use your imagination as you draw. Draw the positive metal ions as spheres with a plus sign (+) in the middle and the electrons as tinier circles with a minus sign (-) in the middle.

Make a collection of different metals. How many common metals are you familiar with? All metals are solids at normal temperatures except one. Do you know what that one metal is? How can it be turned into a solid? How can iron, which is normally a solid, be turned into a liquid?

You can do Surprising Spoon with a fork as well. What other items do you think would work? Can you do this with a paper clip? Why or why not? Can you do it with a table knife? Why or why not?

Imagine you are a metal atom in the handle of a spoon, surrounded on all sides by other metal atoms. Write a description of what you experience as the handle is bent back and forth right at the spot where you are. What do you see around you? What does it feel like? What happens to you as the handle begins to crack?

Draw a cartoon picture of a surprised observer watching a magician bend a spoon with her mind. Put a humorous caption under the cartoon in which the magician makes comments about her psychic powers.

Now You See It, Now You Don't

CHAPTER

5

Physical Properties of Giant Molecules

 Amazing String: Molecular Memory

Dialogue

Paige: I can turn two pieces of string into one.

José: So can I. Just tie them together.

P: No, I mean two into one . . . REALLY, with no knots.

J: You can't do it without knots. You could use tape of course.

P: No. No knots and no tape. I can change two pieces into one.

J: You can't, unless you glue them together.

P: Don't be so sure, José. Look at this. What do you see?

J: A piece of string in a loop, tied at the end. That's not two pieces of string.

P: No, it isn't. It's one. But you can make two. Here's a pair of scissors. Now cut
    the loop in two.

J: Glad to.

[José cuts the loop in half.]

P: Now I'll untie the knot. What do you see now?

J: Two pieces of string. I just cut the loop of string in half.

P: Keep your eye on them, José.

[Paige puts the short ends inside her fist, letting the long ends out either end.]

Pull on the ends of the two pieces, OK?

J: Glad to. Is that enough?

P: Sure!

J: So?

[Paige opens her fist, showing the string whole again.]

   What?

P: Told you I could do it!

J: Let me see that string. How'd you do that?

P: I'm good, José.

J: Tell me how you did it.

P: In my fist. I did it in my fist.

J: But HOW? How did you do it?

P: I just did.

◉ Description

What You Need

1. Some twine (natural Jute twine works best). Try and get twine with two or four twisted strands. Do not use twine with three twisted strands.

2. Scissors

3. White craft glue

How to Do It

Figure 5–1 shows the steps you'll need to follow, which are described below. Take a "single piece of string" about eight to twelve inches long, which has its ends tied together in a knot so that it forms a loop. [This is actually a specially prepared piece of twine. The knot isn't real, and the ends have been glued together. A more complete description and details of the preparation are below in the How It Works section.] Have a friend take a pair of scissors and cut the loop at the end opposite from the knot. Then take the "two" strands, knotted at one end, and untie the knot so that they now appear separate.

Tell your friend that you will now rejoin the cut strings into a whole string. Grab two "ends" of the string, "A" and "B," in your fist as shown (the ends coming from the untied knot). Have your friend pull on the other ends, "X" and "Y," coming from your fist. When they are pulled tight, open your fist and the string is now whole again. Incredible as it seems, the string that was just cut in half by your friend is now a whole string!

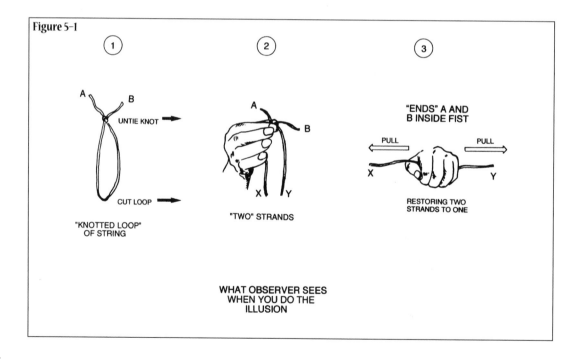

Figure 5-1

1

2

3

A   B
UNTIE KNOT ➡

CUT LOOP ➡

"KNOTTED LOOP"
OF STRING

A

B

X   Y

"TWO" STRANDS

"ENDS" A AND
B INSIDE FIST

PULL ⬅   PULL ➡

X   Y

RESTORING TWO
STRANDS TO ONE

WHAT OBSERVER SEES
WHEN YOU DO THE
ILLUSION

How It Works

The string is prepared beforehand in a special way. Right in the middle of an eight- to-twelve inch piece of twine, pull the two separate spiraled strands apart as shown (Figure 5–2). This can be done easily by twisting the twine so that it unwinds in the middle. Let each part of this untwisted twine coil back on itself as shown so that they reform two strands, A and B, which meet and cross back on the main strand. Tie a loose knot in the two short segments, A and B.

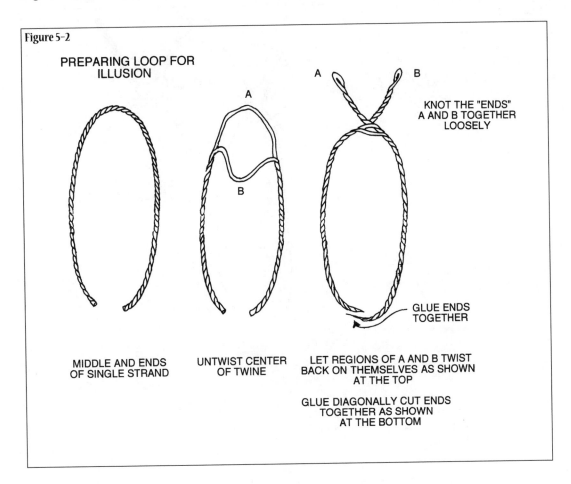

Figure 5-2

PREPARING LOOP FOR
ILLUSION

A

B

A   B

KNOT THE "ENDS"
A AND B TOGETHER
LOOSELY

GLUE ENDS
TOGETHER

MIDDLE AND ENDS
OF SINGLE STRAND

UNTWIST CENTER
OF TWINE

LET REGIONS OF A AND B TWIST
BACK ON THEMSELVES AS SHOWN
AT THE TOP

GLUE DIAGONALLY CUT ENDS
TOGETHER AS SHOWN
AT THE BOTTOM

With a pair of scissors, cut each of the other real ends of the twine on a sharp diagonal. Put a thin film of white craft glue on both of the diagonally cut ends and press them together. You can roll them between your fingers to spread the glue evenly in order to join them. Let the glue dry.

You are now ready to show the "string" to a friend and have him or her cut the big loop using scissors right where you have glued the ends together (Figure 5-3). Now untie the loose knot and hold the twine with your fingers right over the place where the coiled strands cross.

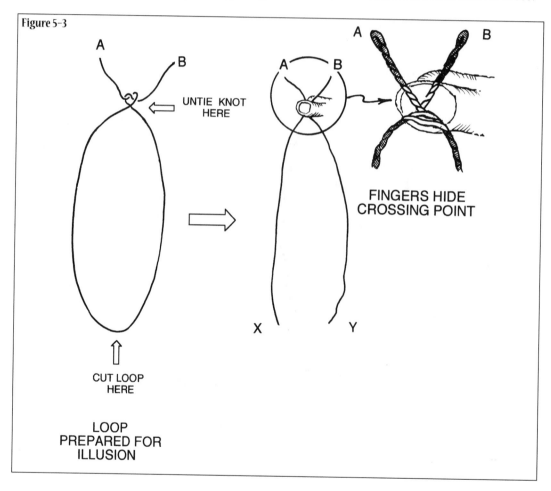

Figure 5-3

A
B

UNTIE KNOT
HERE

A B

A B

FINGERS HIDE
CROSSING POINT

X Y

CUT LOOP
HERE

LOOP
PREPARED FOR
ILLUSION

It appears that you are holding two separate pieces. You can even lay them down on the table (but don't let anyone pick them up). They appear as two separate pieces laying crosswise, one over the other. Of course, right where they cross they are really joined, but that is not apparent at all.

Now grab the "two" pieces at the crossing point, putting both short ends inside your fist and letting the long ends, X and Y, come out either side. Ask the observer to pull on these. When he or she does, the separately coiled strands will be pulled apart, and the twine will recoil back to its original state. It has a kind of "memory" of the way it coils and will always recoil to its original state, a single strand of twine. It may be carefully examined. No one will easily detect what has happened. It is an amazing effect. A cut string appears to have been magically restored, and no one will be able to detect how it occurs.

Variations, Explorations, and Extensions

Try different kinds of twine to see which ones work best. Some twines are simply two twisted strands whereas others have three twisted strands. Which works best? Why? Explain why you can't do this trick with plain string instead of twine.

What makes the strands of twine coil upon themselves? Can you draw a detailed picture of a coil of twine, showing how the strands wrap around each other? What makes a single strand of twine coil upon itself?

Can you make a list of other things that come twisted together? Do you know of any plants that grow in a twisted form? What objects other than twine come in twisted forms?

Why won't this effect work with wire made of twisted strands? What properties of wire are different from twine that would cause it to fail?

What You See and What You Don't

What is actually used in this illusion is not string, but twine. It is best to use the term "string" while you are presenting it to avoid the close similarity of the words *twist* and *twine*. The whole illusion depends on the twisting properties of twine, and it is best to avoid language that might lead the observer to think about this. So the word *string* is used here for issues relating to presentation, whereas the word *twine* is used when we talk about how the illusion is prepared and works.

When unknowing observers see a loop of string with the ends tied together, they rely on their previous experience and automatically assume nothing is odd or strange about what they see. It is right in front of their eyes. If they examined the knot of the tied loop of string very carefully with a magnifying glass, they would be able to see something odd about the knot. The two ends that are tied actually come from the middle of the piece of string. But of course no magnifying glass is available and they are unable to see such details. So they accept the "string" as it appears. And the "string" is presented to them with words which reinforce what they are seeing: "Here is a piece of string tied into a loop" and "Now cut the string in two using these scissors."

The same goes for the diagonally glued ends. If they are glued together properly, nothing will appear odd. The loop of twine appears continuous, except at the knot. So both these effects, the unusual "middle knot" and the glued ends, along with the words noting that this is "just a loop of string," create an illusion: a simple length of string with the ends tied together. Most important, the observers rely on their extensive past experience of what string is. Adding this experience to the perception of what they see in front of them creates in their minds something that really doesn't exist, a whole piece of string tied into a loop.

When the observer cuts the twine with scissors, the experience of creating two pieces from one is profound. There is no way observers can understand that they have cut what you have already glued together. After the loop is cut near the glued region and the knot is untied, the illusion gets even stronger, provided that the observer only sees the crossed strings and *does not handle them.*

The sense of sight alone is insufficient to detect the deception. The single strand appears as two, one laying on top of the other. The fact that they are connected where they cross, and that what is actually being seen is a single piece of twine with twisted strands coming from its center, is not at all apparent. Of course, it would be detected immediately if the "two pieces" of twine were handled, since they can't be separated. They are really a single piece. But observers never get to do that. The twine is quickly restored before they get a chance. Afterwards, they can handle and examine it as much as they like.

Pulling on the cut ends draws the middle twisted strands back out and straightens them. With a slight rotation of the extended twine in the correct direction, these strands will then twist back upon each other, as they were in the original piece of twine. It becomes "whole" again.

The illusion of restoration is most profound because the observer pulls on the ends of the string, totally unaware that pulling the ends X and Y in opposite directions is the cause of the straightening and retwisting process that results in the restored single strand. This is real magic at its best.

To get this illusion just right requires a bit of practice, particularly at the last step where the cut ends are pulled. The twine must be allowed to reform the original spiral twist, and you can help this with some turning by hand. It will simply look like you are rubbing the twine to "rejoin" it. Practice a few times before you try it out on a friend.

◉ A Deeper Look

The effects seen in this illusion depend completely on the twisting properties of twine. When a single strand of twine is pulled straight and then released, it retwists back toward its original twisted state. The giant polymer molecules in the stretched strand have, in a way, a molecular memory of the twisted arrangement. They return to this arrangement when the stretching force is removed. If you pull a thick twisted copper wire out straight, it won't retwist when you let go. It stays straight. Copper metal and twine are different substances with different molecular and atomic properties. The metal atoms in copper wire are quite different from the polymer molecules in the cellulose of twine. (For more details on the structure of metals, see the Deeper Look section of Surprising Spoon.)

Twine is usually made of plant structural material, such as jute. All plant structural material is composed of cellulose, a giant molecule composed of many smaller sugar molecules all attached together. The sugar that makes cellulose is called *glucose*. Many small glucose molecules attached to each other in a chain make up the giant, cellulose polymer molecule. A single giant cellulose molecule is like a long flat ribbon. Many of these single molecular ribbons lying alongside each other result in a single microscopic fiber of cellulose. Many microscopic fibers together, along with some other substances, result in a visible strand of jute. These strands of jute may be twisted together to form a larger strand, called twine. When they are twisted the cellulose ribbons arrange themselves in a specific stable arrangement. When pulled, however, the twisted fibers can be uncoiled, yielding longer, untwisted strands of jute. When the pulling force is released, the strands retwist and the fiber returns to a semblance of its original state.

In twine, there are two or more main strands, each of which is twisted around the other. As you separate them into untwisted single strands in the middle of the twine and then let each single strand retwist upon itself, the jute fibers are simply uncoiling and then recoiling.

◎ Questions to Draw and Write About

Many kinds of natural, giant polymer molecules are different types of twisted coils, just like twine. However, the twists are too small to see, much smaller than the twists in twine. The protein in hair is one type of molecular coil. It exists in what is called an alpha helix, a single coiled strand, similar to a spring. Many single alpha helixes together result in strands of protein in a single hair on your head.

The genetic material in a cell nucleus, called DNA, is another type of giant polymer molecule. It exists in a twisted form like twine, called a double helix. Many molecules of DNA combine to form a gene, a coded sequence of molecules that make up a chromosome in the cell.

Get a biology book from your library and see if you can find more information and pictures of these giant twisted molecules, as well as more information about protein and cellulose chains. Draw pictures of each and label them. Would they become longer if stretched? Might they retwist if the stretching force was removed?

Just as twine can be untwisted in the middle to create the illusion Amazing String, DNA untwists in the middle when it controls the formation of other molecules important in growth and reproduction of cells (Figure 5–4).

Metal springs can be good models for some kinds of coiled polymer chains. Write a paragraph describing the ways in which a spring is like a giant polymer molecule. Use the descriptions of polymers you find in the biology book.

There is a lot of deception and misleading language needed to successfully perform the illusion Amazing String. Look over the dialogue between Paige and José. How many instances can you find where Paige misleads José? What do you think would happen if Paige tried to do the illusion a second time for him? Would he let her do everything the same way as before, or would he ask different questions and ask to see different things? Write down a list of all the things you think José might do to find out how the string was restored.

Imagine that you are a twisted strand of twine. Write a brief description of what it might be like if you were stretched out so that your twists "unwound" and became straight. How does it feel to be coiled? How does it feel to be straight?

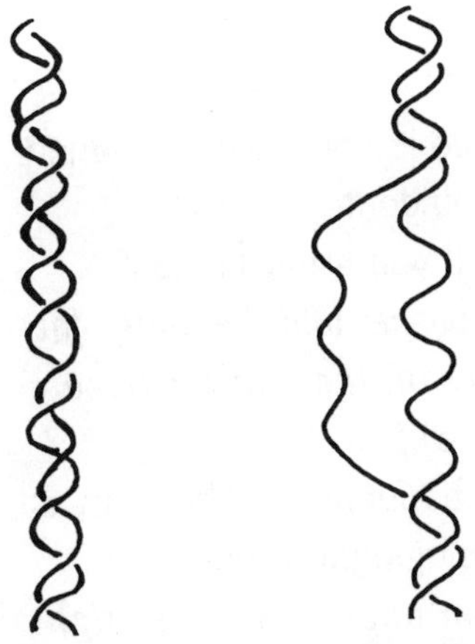

Draw a cartoon strip showing two people trying to understand how the illusion Amazing String works. Show them very puzzled and have them make statements that show how confused they are.

Figure 5-4

DOUBLE TWISTED
STRAND OF
DNA

DOUBLE TWISTED STRAND
OF DNA UNTWISTED
IN THE CENTER

Unbelievable Quarter: Seeing Through Molecules

◎ Dialogue

José: Hey Amber, look at this quarter sitting on top of the piece of rubber I've stretched over a glass.

Amber: I see it. What did you put it there for?

J: Take your finger and push down on the quarter.

A: Why?

J: Just do it. You'll see why when you do it.

A: OK! If you want, I'll do it.

[Amber pushes with her index finger on the quarter (Figure 5–5).]

What's happening? The coin is going right through. . . .

[The coin appears to pass right through the stretched rubber and drops into the covered glass.]

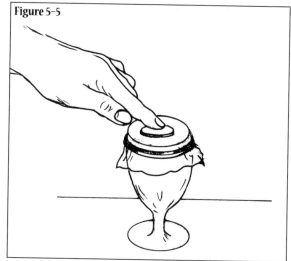

Figure 5-5

J: What do you see now?

A: The coin went right through into the glass. How is that possible? You must have cut a hole in the rubber.

J: Nope. Take a look at it.

[Amber looks carefully at the rubber covering the glass.]

A: I don't see how that could happen. What kind of rubber is that? How did the quarter get through it into the glass?

J: Just a piece I cut from a balloon. I covered the glass with it and put a quarter on top. Then you pressed on it.

A: But how did it go through?

J: Magic!

A: Come on, José. How did it do that?

J: It's a special quarter that can drop through things.

A: No, it isn't. It's just a regular quarter.

[Amber takes the quarter out of the glass and examines it carefully.]

J: Well—it's really a special kind of rubber that stuff can drop right through.

A: Come on, José. It isn't. My finger won't go through it. Tell me how it works.

J: I'll tell you tomorrow.

A: Why not now?

J: Tomorrow.

◉ Description

What You Need

1. A very large *colorless* balloon (a party store or toy store can order these if they have none in stock). The ballon must have a translucent, off-yellow color, the color of natural rubber.

2. A small, heavy-walled glass with a relatively small top

3. A pair of scissors

4. A quarter (other coins will also work well)

5. Some rubber bands

6. A pill bottle or other narrow container

How to Do It

Put the bottom blade of the scissors inside the uninflated balloon. Cut the balloon down the side from the top to the bottom so you can open it up. Cut out the largest piece of rubber you can from the open balloon.

Put a quarter on top of a narrow container, such as a pill bottle or lipstick case, so that it covers the top completely. Hold the piece of rubber on the sides, stretch it out above the quarter, and place the center over the quarter on the top of the container. Now push the rubber down with your hands, stretching it over the quarter and the container. You should cover the coin tightly with the stretched rubber as shown (Figure 5–6).

Bring your thumbs in underneath the quarter and then release the rubber. The coin will now be stuck in the center of the piece of rubber. The top surface and sides of the coin will

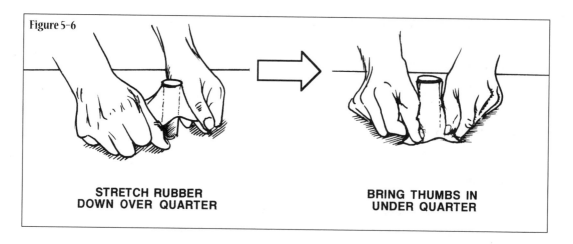

Figure 5-6

STRETCH RUBBER DOWN OVER QUARTER

BRING THUMBS IN UNDER QUARTER

be clearly visible through the stretched rubber, which goes over the top side and bunches up underneath the bottom of the coin (Figure 5–7).

Take the coin in the rubber, covered side up, and gently stretch the rubber over the top of a narrow-mouthed glass. Hold the rubber on the glass with rubber bands. Stretch it tightly over the glass, but not so tightly that the coin is forced out.

Now you can show this setup to a friend. It appears clearly and unmistakably to an observer as a coin sitting on top of a piece of rubber, which is stretched over the top of a glass. Have your friend push down on the coin with a finger. It will feel like touching the coin itself.

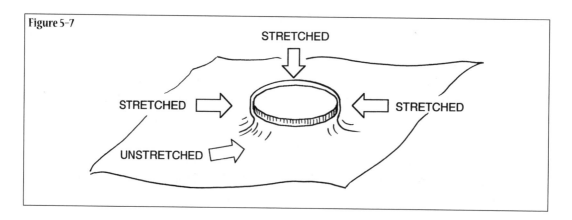

Figure 5-7

STRETCHED

STRETCHED

STRETCHED

UNSTRETCHED

As your friend presses on the coin, it "drops through the rubber" into the glass. The visual effect is startling. It appears that the coin sitting on top of the rubber has passed right through it into the glass.

How It Works

The illusion works because of several properties of natural rubber. First, it is translucent, and the coin seen through the rubber does not seem covered by anything. The effect is enhanced because the stretched rubber goes from the top of the coin down the sides and underneath it, holding it in place. Because of this, both the edges and top of the coin are clearly visible. Because the vertical sides are so clearly apparent, the coin appears to be sitting on the stretched rubber, rather than underneath it. This is confirmed by the sense of touch, which is unable to distinguish between touching a thin sheet of rubber over a coin and touching the coin itself.

When a finger puts pressure on the top surface of the rubber and the coin underneath, the rubber bunched up under the coin gives way, and the coin is released into the glass. Of course it already is "in" the glass; it's just held up by the stretched rubber. This is completely undetectable.

Both the sense of sight and touch are fooled. The illusion is superb.

Variations, Explorations, and Extensions

Try the effect with various coins to see which works best. If you have trouble finding a colorless balloon, try using colored balloons and plastic tiddledywinks of the same color (these are available in most toy stores).

You can vary the effect by filling the glass with water and letting the coin or tiddledywink fall into it. However, part of the startling effect is the sound of the coin dropping into the glass, and this will be diminished by the water.

Can you find other objects that will work just as well as coins? Will a key work, or does the object have to be circular? If it does, why is that? Try the effect with two coins stacked one on top of the other. Will two stacked dimes work? How about two stacked quarters? A bottle cap, face up, works nicely; but it can cut the rubber that is over it. Give it a try and see what you think.

◉ What You See and What You Don't

This illusion is one of best in the book. The sensations of sight, touch, and sound are all fooled. Not very many illusions can fool all three.

The illusion of the quarter sitting on top of the rubber is fixed in the mind of the observer for several reasons. Because the balloon has no pigment in the rubber, it becomes so translucent when stretched thin that the coin is seen right through it. The top of the quarter is seen directly. The sides of the quarter are also seen sticking up from the surface, a very convincing bit of evidence supporting the illusion of a three-dimensional coin on a flat surface. In addition, the sense of touch doesn't help correct the misapprehension; it reinforces it. The coin itself is "felt" directly, and the thin film of rubber covering it is not noticed.

Add to all of this the sound of the coin clinking when it drops into the glass, and it is clear that what you see, touch, and hear are all misleading sensations. How could the coin already be "in" the glass when you hear the clink of it dropping down after you see it sitting on the top of the rubber? This contradiction is impossible to understand unless you know what is happening.

This illusion must not be done more than once!!! And the first time it is done, you must simply ask the observers to press on the coin they see. You need not tell them what will happen. They will be surprised enough when it does. If you try to do it again, observers will attempt to pick up the coin from the surface of the rubber, and everything is revealed immediately. Once understood, the magic is gone. So even under intense questioning, you should NEVER reveal what has happened. You can make up stories about the "special coin" or the "special kind of rubber," but keep the real information to yourself. As noted in Surprising Spoon, if you tell how the illusion is done, your observers will be greatly disappointed, and you will simply become a liar.

On the other hand, observers can examine the coin, glass, and rubber as much as they want after you have done the illusion one time. It is very difficult for anyone, even a very observant scientist, to understand what has happened. Sight and touch have been interpreted incorrectly, and sound has reinforced these misinterpretations (both the language of presentation and the clinking of the coin in the glass). And there is no clue in the objects themselves that leads to an easy explanation.

⊙ A Deeper Look

Rubber is made of giant polymer molecules, long linked chains of small molecules. A molecule is a specific number of particular kinds of atoms, connected together in a particular pattern. Giant polymer molecules are much larger than small molecules like sugar or water, but they are still too small to see. They are similar to the giant molecules of protein that compose muscle or the giant molecules of cellulose that compose plant structural material (the framework of stems and leaves).

The elastic properties of rubber can be explained by the special structure of its long chains. You can't stretch a water or sugar molecule, or other small molecules, but rubber can be stretched because its long chains are coiled and tangled together. When pulled, they uncoil and untangle themselves, and become longer. When released, they recoil and retangle again (Figure 5–8).

The twisted, long polymer molecules in a piece of rubber from a balloon can elongate dramatically when the rubber is stretched. The one property of rubber that is essential in Amazing Quarter is its ability to return to its original unstretched length when the stretching forces are removed. There are many substances with properties like this. They are called *elastomers* and the property that allows them to be stretched and then return to their original state is called *elasticity*. Elasticity is a direct result of the uncoiling and untangling of long

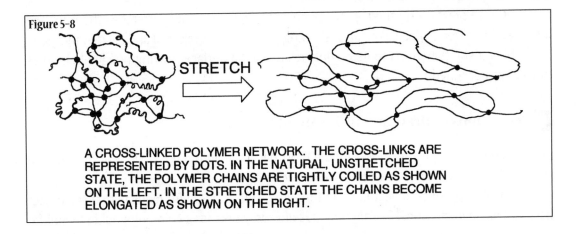

Figure 5-8

STRETCH

A CROSS-LINKED POLYMER NETWORK. THE CROSS-LINKS ARE
REPRESENTED BY DOTS. IN THE NATURAL, UNSTRETCHED
STATE, THE POLYMER CHAINS ARE TIGHTLY COILED AS SHOWN
ON THE LEFT. IN THE STRETCHED STATE THE CHAINS BECOME
ELONGATED AS SHOWN ON THE RIGHT.

polymer chains and the ability of these to retangle and recoil when the force holding the chains in their elongated state is removed.

In a piece of rubber balloon that is in a relaxed, unstretched state, the tangled molecules are very disordered. When the rubber is stretched, the molecules become elongated in the direction of the stretch, but they still remain in similar positions relative to one another and cannot slide past each other because of the crosslinking connections (the dots in Figure 5–8). When the force causing the stretching is removed, the molecules return to their original tangled states, and the stretched rubber rapidly shrinks back to it original length.

The more crosslinks that are in an elastomer, the less elastic it becomes. If there are too many crosslinks, the material changes into an unstretchable solid. If there are too few, it becomes a very *viscous liquid*. A viscous liquid is one that pours very slowly, such as cold honey or very cold motor oil. Just the right amount of crosslinks will result in a rubbery material that is neither a rigid solid nor a thick liquid. The rubber of balloons has just the right number of crosslinks.

When the rubber is stretched over the top of the quarter and pulled down around it, the thin film that forms over the top and down the sides of the coin has elongated rubber molecules in it. When the stretched rubber is released from the bottom, the stretched part is caught by the sides of the coin, and the rubber bunches up underneath it. The bunched-up rubber has returned to its unstretched state on the bottom of the coin. This arrangement traps the quarter in the sheet of rubber.

Putting pressure on the top of the coin through the rubber stretches the bunched rubber at the bottom, which elongates, allowing the coin to be released and fall into the glass. The rubber instantly returns to its original relatively flat surface, leaving no clue behind as to what has occurred.

◉ Questions to Draw and Write About

This illusion and Surprising Spoon are the most deceptive in the book. Do you agree or disagree with this statement? In writing, explain your position.

The illusion of an object passing through a thin rubber film requires that the object have certain characteristics. Explain why this illusion works for a coin but wouldn't work for a marble, a paper clip, or a pencil stub. What characteristics of the coin make it work so well? Why would a round eraser in the shape of a coin work less well?

Explain why it feels like you are touching the coin when you are really touching the rubber film. Rubber is not at all like metal. Why does the observer "feel the coin" when he or she is really touching the stretched rubber?

What would happen if you used a colored balloon with a quarter in this illusion? Would your observer detect what happens? Why or why not?

Draw a detailed, magnified picture of a coin caught up in a rubber film as happens in this illusion.

Pretend you are small enough to sit in the bottom of a small glass that is covered with the film of rubber and embedded coin. Look up at the quarter above your head and write a brief description of what you see. Draw a picture of what you see. Write a description of what you would see if someone pressed on the rubber over the coin and it fell into the glass.

Imagine that you are a quarter embedded in a thin film of rubber stretched over the top of a glass. Write a brief description of what is holding you up. What does it feel like? Look up and describe what you see. Look down and describe what you see.

Draw a cartoon of a scientist pushing a coin through a film of rubber stretched over a glass. Try and show the scientist's surprise and amazement when the coin drops down into the glass. Think of a humorous caption to put beneath the cartoon.

CHAPTER 6

Surface Sorcery
Topology and Chirality

 Crazy Cloth: Topological Twists

🎯 **Dialogue**

Paige: See these three loops of cloth?

José : What are they for?

P: Watch me cut one down the middle with scissors (Figure 6–1).

J: What are you doing it for?

P: I'm making two loops from this one.

J: Why, Paige? What for?

P: Let's see you do it with one. I'll bet you can't.

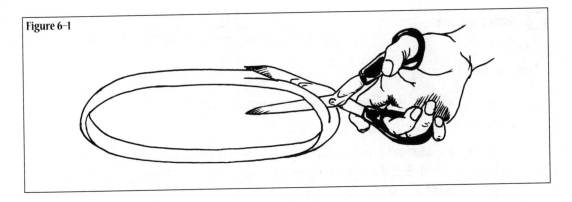
Figure 6–1

J: Of course I can. Give me the scissors.

[José takes the second loop and cuts it just as Paige cut the first loop.]

What happened? It didn't work!

P: You just made a bigger loop.

J: But I cut it just like you did. How come I got only one loop and you got two?

P: I said you couldn't do it.

J: I can too. Let me try it again with the last one.

P: OK. Here it is.

[José cuts his second loop down the middle.]

J: Well . . . I got two loops. But they're attached to each other. How come? This is very strange. You got two separate loops, and I got one large one the first time I did it and two connected loops the second time. I don't get it.

P: Maybe you didn't cut it like I did.

J: I did so. Right down the middle.

P: Maybe my cuts are more accurate that yours.

J: That has nothing to do with it. Something is very odd.

P: Yes, I guess it is.

◉ Description

What You Need

1. An old sheet, pillowcase, or some other cotton cloth
2. A pair of scissors
3. Some iron-on cloth bonding tape, such as Stitch Witchery (manufactured by Dritz) or HeatnBond (manufactured by Therm O Web). These products can be purchased at any fabric store.

How to Do It

Show your friends the three loops, A, B, and C. Tell them to watch carefully as you cut one down the center. Use loop A. When you are finished, you will have two loops. Each is the same diameter as the original. Now challenge your friends to do the same. Give them one of the other loops and the scissors. Let's say they choose loop B. Cutting it down the center yields one large loop twice as big as the original. Ask if they wish to try again. Cutting loop C yields two interlocking loops. They might choose C first and then try again with B, but it really doesn't matter. They can't duplicate what you did and produce two separate loops from one. Instead they produce either one large loop or two linked loops (Figure 6–2).

How It Works

Cut three strips of cloth, each about an inch wide and three-feet long. Take one strip and make a loop, overlapping the ends about a quarter of an inch. Place a small piece of the bonding tape between the overlapped sections. Apply a hot iron to the overlapped region to bond the ends together. We'll call this loop A. Do the same thing with the second strip to create a second loop, but before you overlap and bond the ends, twist the strip once. We'll call this loop B. Finally, do the same thing with the third strip. But before you overlap and bond the ends, twist this third strip twice. We'll call this loop C. (See Figure 6–3).

When loop A is cut down the center, it yields two loops with diameters identical to loop A, as you might expect. Loop B is a special kind of cloth loop called a *Möbius strip*. Such a loop formed because you twisted the cloth before bonding the ends together. It has only one edge and one surface. Because of this, it has special properties that cause the loop, when cut down the middle, to yield only a single new loop twice as big as the original. In a similar fashion, loop C—with two twists—has unique properties. When cut down the middle it results in two interlocking loops, the same diameter as the original.

Though this effect can be done using paper strips, the resulting loops are more clearly seen as different. The rigidity of the paper highlights the untwisted nature of A and the twisted shapes of B and C.

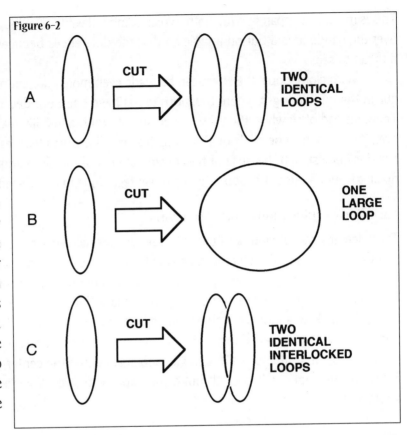

Figure 6-2

A — CUT → TWO IDENTICAL LOOPS

B — CUT → ONE LARGE LOOP

C — CUT → TWO IDENTICAL INTERLOCKED LOOPS

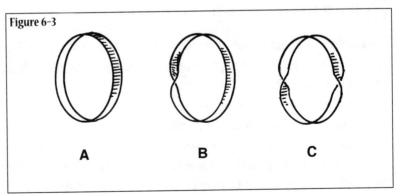

Figure 6-3

A   B   C

This is much less apparent with cloth, which is more flexible. The loops are more easily hung over the hands or laid out on a table so that the differences between A, B, and C are very difficult to see.

With cloth loops, the effect can be made even more dramatic by starting with a small cut in the middle, right where the cloth loops have been bonded with the iron-on tape. Then, instead of slowly cutting the looped strip down the middle, tear it. If you tear it, however, the loops must be made of a cloth such as muslin, which tears easily. The tear in muslin remains quite straight because of the thread patterns of the cloth and will meet itself as you rip all the way around the loop. The rapid tear technique makes the effect more startling.

Variations, Explorations, and Extensions

Try different kinds of cloth and paper to see which ones work best. With paper strips, you can make the loops with glue or transparent tape. Instead of cutting loop B down the center, cut it near one edge, keeping the scissors the same distance from the edge as you cut. You will produce a small loop interlocked with a large loop.

Try making a loop with three twists in it instead of two. What happens when you cut this down the center? Can you figure out why? The result might be called a single loop with a "knot" in it. If you cut this single loop again down the center, including through the center of the paper as it goes through the paper knot, you'll get a single loop with two knots in it.

◉ What You See and What You Don't

The key to this effect is the twisting of the strips before they are bonded together to form loops. If this is done with paper loops, especially those made from short paper strips, the twisting is clearly obvious. An observer will easily notice that A, B, and C are not at all the same kind of loops. While observers may still be puzzled about how these differently prepared loops, when cut down the middle, yield three different results, it will be obvious that it has something to do with the twists. Try this with glued paper loops and see.

The use of long cloth strips avoids this problem because the twists are hidden in the folds and normal twists of flexible cotton. You can hold each loop of cloth in your right and left hands, pulling it out to show the respective loops. As the cloth passes through your fingers, you can compress it a bit, so that what an observer sees is simply a band of cloth, much like a loop of rope or string. The twists are hidden.

The hidden twists in the loop are also obscured by the language used to present the effect. In the dialogue between Paige and José, the loops are presented as identical. It is best not to say explicitly that they are "identical," because using this term will immediately raise suspicion that they are not. So don't lie, at least not about the identity of the strips. You can be a much more creative liar later, as noted in the next paragraph. Let the observer assume that they are identical. Once they are split, there is no way to go back and check.

You can improvise in many other ways as well. For instance, you can take three small cardboard tubes from toilet paper or paper towels. These might even be painted different colors. On one draw two circles with a marking pen. On another, draw a larger circle. On the last, draw two interconnected circles. You can pull cloth A through the first tube before you tear it, cloth B through the second, and C through the third. During this process, you can talk about how these tubes affect the molecular structure of cellulose in the cloth by imposing an electromagnetic field on the hydrogen bonds in the cloth, altering the helical arrangement of the force fields . . . etc., etc., blah, blah. You get the idea, don't you?

◎ A Deeper Look

This effect is based on the topological properties of the various twisted loops and has been used by magicians since the latter part of the last century. Topology is the study of the properties of surfaces. More familiar terms are *topography,* usually referring to the surface of a part of the earth, and *topographical,* as in a topographical map, which details the heights of the mapped regions with altitude lines. More specifically, in mathematics, topology is the study of those properties of geometric figures that do not change at all when the figure itself is subjected to continuous change.

For example, loop A has two surfaces, an inside one and an outside one. The two loops produced when A is split both have that same property, an inside and outside surface. This can be verified by coloring the inside and outside surfaces of A with different colored pens and looking at the colors in the loops produced by the splitting.

Loop B has only one surface. This can also be verified with a colored marker. The large loop that results from the splitting of B has this same property as well, which can be verified by looking at the color of split loop B.

Loop C has two surfaces, just like loop A. This can again be verified using colored markers. Splitting it results in two interconnected loops, each of which has two surfaces, just like the original.

The first description of the properties of a surface like that on strip B was by a German astronomer, Augustus Möbius, and strips such as B have become known as Möbius strips. The effects of cutting Möbius strips with one or more twists has been used in magic for many years. In the early part of the century, the effect using paper rings was called "The Afghan Bands." An interesting short history of the effect is summarized by Martin Gardner in his book *Mathematics, Magic and Mystery* (see Appendix B).

◉ Questions to Draw and Write About

After you try this effect on friends, ask them to make a list of questions they would like to ask you about it. After they write down their lists, ask them to write a paragraph explaining how they think the effect works. Read their paragraphs and see if you think they are on the right track.

Make loops A, B, and C out of twelve-inch strips of paper that are each about one inch wide. Color each inside and outside surface of each loop with a different-colored marker. If there is only one surface, you will use only one color. If there are two, you should use two different colors.

Write careful descriptions of the paper loops A, B, and C that you made. You should also include a careful diagram of each, using the colored markers to show the colors as they actually appear. Your verbal descriptions should be as accurate as possible. Try very carefully to represent the three-dimensional properties of the strips in your two-dimensional diagrams.

Now cut each of the loops down the middle. Write a detailed description of the result. Make a careful drawing of the results as well, coloring in the surfaces as you see them.

Go to an encyclopedia in your library or to an on-line computer service if you have one, and look up the term *topology*. See if you find anything of interest. Try to find the origin of the prefix *topo*, the beginning of the words *topology* and *topography*. Is it of Greek or Latin origin? What is its meaning? Can you see how it relates to topology and topography?

Write a story about a person who is walking over a river on a bridge that is similar to a Möbius loop. Have the person look down below and see the river. After the person walks awhile, the river is above and part of the bridge previously walked upon is below. Of course, this will be a story of fantasy, because the water would fall on the person's head, and he or she would fall off the bridge. But don't worry about that. Be creative. Try to imagine what walking on a Möbius path would be like. Draw a picture to go along with your story.

Draw a cartoon strip of a talking Möbius loop. Have the loop describe itself to a regular loop that is listening and asking questions. Try to create a humorous and lively interaction between the two. You might even want to have the Möbius loop split itself down the center and have the resulting parts take part in the conversation.

 ## Upside Down: A Folding Inversion

🎯 Dialogue

Bobby: José, I can make the picture of George Washington on a dollar bill jump upside down.

José: What do you mean, "jump upside down"?

B: See his picture on the bill? All I'm going to do is fold the bill up and then unfold it. And his picture will come out upside down.

J: No, it won't.

B: Just watch very carefully. First, I'm folding it up from the bottom.

J: OK.

B: Now I'm folding it over. And then over one more time (Figure 6–4).

J: OK. Now what?

Figure 6-4

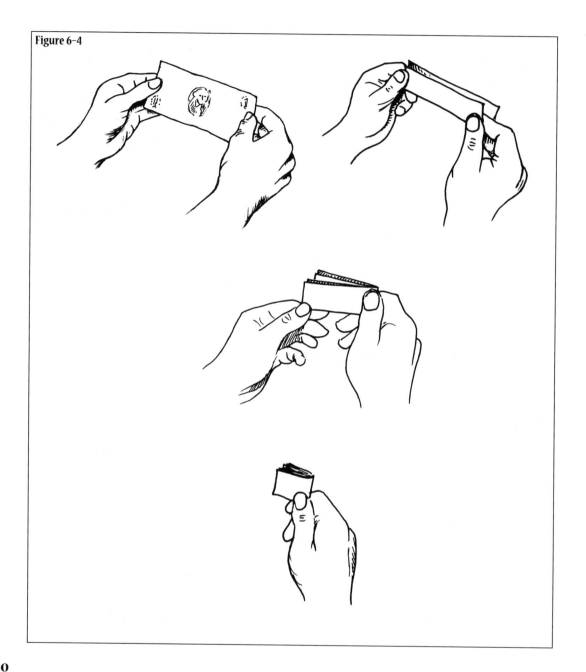

B: I'm going to very slowly open it up just like I folded it, once, twice, and then back down, just like I started (Figure 6–5).

J: And?

B: Look!

J: It is upside down. How can that have happened?

B: I'm good at folding magic, José.

J: You aren't. And folding isn't magic anyway. Do it again.

B: OK. Watch carefully now so you don't miss anything.

[Bobby repeats the whole sequence and the bill again comes out upside down.]

J: Let me try that.

B: Sure. Go ahead. Fold it up and then open it up like you folded it, just like I did. But remember, you haven't got my magic touch.

[José tries and it doesn't work.]

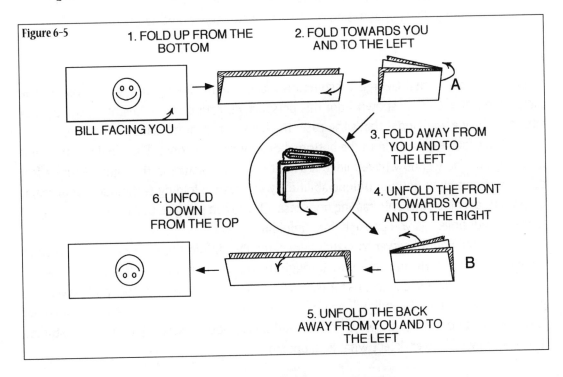

Figure 6-5

1. FOLD UP FROM THE BOTTOM

2. FOLD TOWARDS YOU AND TO THE LEFT

A

BILL FACING YOU

3. FOLD AWAY FROM YOU AND TO THE LEFT

6. UNFOLD DOWN FROM THE TOP

4. UNFOLD THE FRONT TOWARDS YOU AND TO THE RIGHT

5. UNFOLD THE BACK AWAY FROM YOU AND TO THE LEFT

B

J: I don't understand how you did it.

B: I'm very talented, José.

J: Come on, show me.

B: But I did show you. Just do it exactly like I did it!

[José keeps trying while Bobby looks on.]

⊙ Description

What You Need

1. A dollar bill

2. Any rectangular piece of paper about the size of a dollar bill will work as well if you put a directional design on it such as an arrow pointing up

How to Do It

Hold a dollar bill so that George Washington's face is right side up and facing you. All the pictures in Figure 6–5 are shown from this perspective. Your observer might be standing or sitting alongside you, and if that's the case, the bill will appear the same way to them.

Now, fold the bill up from the bottom, horizontally, as shown. Then fold it in half, and in half again. You will now have folded it as in the middle picture in the figure. Pause a few seconds to comment on your unique abilities, your creative folding techniques, your magical powers, or some other entertaining nonsense. Or you can just give the folded bill a "magic" tap with your finger, as you pause before unfolding it.

Now tell your observer to watch very carefully. Unfold the bill exactly as shown in the figure. Move slowly and smoothly through the unfolding sequence. It appears to be the reverse of the folding sequence, but it isn't. (Practice before doing this for an observer.) As shown in the diagram, the bill will be upside down when you open up the final horizontal fold. You can't go wrong! It always works! And unless your observer has seen and studied it before, they will never detect what is happening.

How It Works

The key to this effect is in the folding and unfolding sequence. You fold A to get the triple-folded bill (the middle picture in the figure). But you unfold this triple-folded bill to get B, which is the *mirror image of A*. The folding of A and the unfolding to get B are not the reverse of each other. This results in the mirror image relationship between A and B. It will also be obvious from Figure 6–6 that a right-side-up and upside-down bill, the beginning and end of the whole process, are also mirror images.

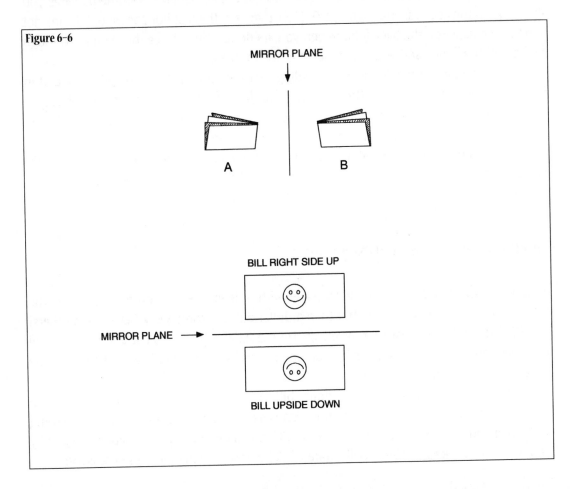

Figure 6–6

Examine all these moves very carefully and you will see how this inversion occurs. The interesting part of this effect is that only a very astute observer will notice the different sequence of folding and unfolding. When you unfold the bill in a mirror-image sequence, the sequence is not easily detected.

To see more clearly how it works, cut out a piece of white paper the same size as a dollar bill. Put a large ink mark in the middle of the top edge of the front of the paper, a little to the left of the center. This would be near the top of Washington's head if you had put an ink mark on a bill. The ink should be visible through the paper. Now fold the paper as you did the bill in the above sequence to get A. Note that after the first horizontal fold the ink dot is inside the paper on the back fold. When you are done, you will see the ink mark through the back of the paper, and you will notice it is still on the top.

Now, continue the folding and unfolding sequence from A to B. You will note that in B the ink spot, though still on the top, is on the front fold, facing inward. You have, in effect, turned the horizontally folded paper over. So when you continue to unfold and open it up, the front goes down and the ink dot is at the bottom.

Try this effect with several different pieces of paper, putting ink dots on several different regions of the paper so you can see more clearly how the mirror image sequence affects the outcome.

Variations, Explorations, and Extensions

Try different-sized pieces of rectangular paper with different designs on them to see if you can make one that works even better than a dollar bill. Do some work better than others? Why? Are there designs that ruin the effect? For example, if you put a circle in the center of the paper, can you see the inversion? What properties of a circle are different from the picture of George Washington? How does this alter the effect?

What happens if you unfold a dollar bill exactly the same way you folded it? Can you draw a detailed picture of both of these processes? Create a series of pictures showing the folding and unfolding process in each case. Can you describe what is happening just by writing or do you need pictures to illustrate it? Why or why aren't pictures necessary?

⦿ What You See and What You Don't

The effect produced in Upside Down results because the observer does not detect the difference between the folding sequence and the unfolding sequence. The folding and unfolding look the same. They aren't. The folding of A takes place in three-dimensional space in one direction, whereas the unfolding to B takes place in the mirror image of that three-dimensional space. The observer's attention is on the bill itself and the folds. The direction in space of folding and unfolding is not attended to. You can prove this to yourself quickly by unfolding the triple-folded bill in *exactly the same way you folded it from A*. You will get back A, not B. And if you continue on, the image on the bill does not turn upside down at the end of the sequence.

A related kind of effect occurs when we look at ourselves in the mirror. We look perfectly normal, and in fact our reflection is the way we come to know ourselves. We never see us as others do. They see us, not our reflection. In our reflection, right and left are reversed. Our right hand is our reflection's left, and our reflection's left is our right. We really never attend to this because our bodies are, for the most part, symmetrical. There is a vertical plane of symmetry down the middle of us. But if we happen to be wearing a T-shirt with words on it, we notice immediately that something is different in the reflection. The words don't look the same in the mirror as they do on the shirt we read directly. They aren't symmetrical, and they come out looking strange in the reflection.

Some of the folding and unfolding processes in Upside Down are like this. They are not identical. This isn't easily noticed until the bill is finally opened up at the end and we see the overall effect of the nonidentical folding and unfolding processes.

⦿ A Deeper Look

The effect in Upside Down is simply the result of turning a piece of paper over in a rather complex and confusing way. Fold a horizontally held rectangular piece of paper in half as follows: Take the right-hand side and fold it toward you on top of the left-hand side. The fold will now be on your right and the open part on your left. Now unfold it by taking the bottom left and unfolding it away from you. You will see that the open piece of paper has simply been turned over. You are now looking at the back of the page you started with. A similar sort of folding and unfolding happens in Upside Down. However, because there are more folds, it's a bit more complicated. It's harder to see what happens.

After a single piece of paper is folded once toward you, as noted above, it can be unfolded in one of two ways. The front can be unfolded toward you (this returns the paper to its original position) or the back can be unfolded away from you (this turns the paper over.) These processes are mirror images of each other. If the paper is blank on both sides, the end result looks the same: An open piece of blank paper. However, if the front side of the paper has an image, color, or some other identifying difference from the back, then the processes will give different results. Unfolding it toward you exposes the original side of the paper. Unfolding it away from you exposes the backside. There is no magic in this. Anyone can see exactly what is happening. But if you make it more complicated by folding in several different directions and by folding three times instead of once, it isn't so obvious.

To see even more clearly what is happening, try the effect with two large pieces of blank 8½-by-11-inch typing paper, each with a simple smiley face drawn on the front. With both smiley faces facing you and with the long part of the paper horizontal, fold each paper up from the bottom horizontally, as you did with the dollar bill. Take either of these folded papers, TURN THEM OVER, and then unfold them down from the top (exactly the reverse of the way you folded them). The smiley faces will appear upside down.

Instead of just turning the papers over after the first fold, as above, you can make some more complicated folds to turn the faces upside down. First, with the long part of the open papers horizontal again, fold each up from the bottom horizontally, as you did before. Now make another fold, this time vertical, down the middle of each, folding toward you from right to left. Repeat that move again, taking the folded right edge and folding each paper again vertically down the middle, toward you from right to left.

For one of the folded papers, we'll call it A, unfold the last fold toward you exactly the reverse of the way you folded it. Unfold the last fold of the other paper, which we'll call B, away from you. You will notice that A and B are mirror images of each other. Now unfold the remaining vertical fold in A toward you, and lay the horizontally folded paper face up on the table. Now unfold the remaining vertical fold in B away from you, and lay the horizontally folded paper face up on the table. When you open up A and B, the smiley face in

A is up, and in B it is upside down. You can clearly see that opening the second vertical fold in B toward you instead of away from you will turn the smiley face right-side-up again.

Mirror images are very interesting and can be quite complicated. There are two kinds of mirror image relationships. Some mirror images are identical to themselves, and some are not. For example, your left and right hands are mirror images of each other, but they are not *superimposable* on each other (Figure 6–7). The mirror image of your right hand is not identical to your right hand. The same is true for your left hand and its mirror image. That's why you can't fit your right hand into your left glove or your left hand into your right glove. Your feet are the same way. Your right foot doesn't fit in your left shoe and your left foot does not fit in your right shoe. Objects that are not superimposable on their mirror images in this way are said to be *chiral*. Examples of chiral objects include hands, feet, gloves, shoes, spirals, and many other kinds of objects. The word chiral comes from the Greek word for *hand*.

The other kind of mirror image is one that *is* superimposable on itself. It is identical

Figure 6–7

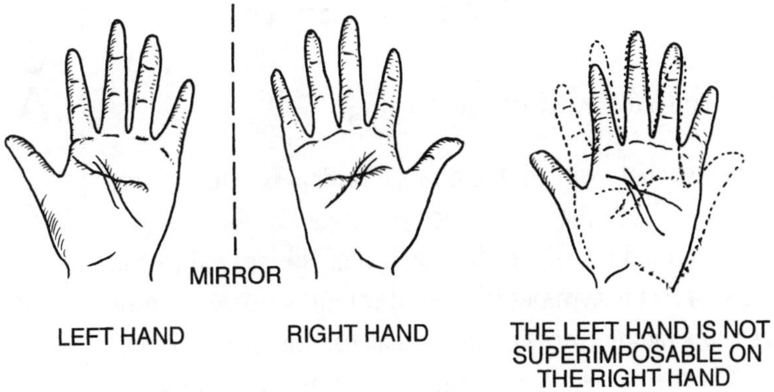

MIRROR

LEFT HAND   RIGHT HAND   THE LEFT HAND IS NOT
                                       SUPERIMPOSABLE ON
                                       THE RIGHT HAND

HANDS AS MODELS OF CHIRAL OBJECTS

to its mirror image. An example would be a ball or a cube. A ball and a cube each have a plane of symmetry that passes directly through their centers. One half is identical to the other half, and so the mirror images may be superimposed on each other. Hands and feet are not like this. They do not have a plane of symmetry. A thumb is on one side of the plane dividing a hand in half, a little finger is on the other. A big toe is on one side of the plane dividing a foot in half, a little toe is on the other.

Letters have similar kinds of symmetry properties that are seen when words are reflected in a mirror. For example, consider the two names in Figure 6–8 as they are written. If you hold them up to a mirror, the boy's name is unchanged, but the girl's name is reversed. As a magician, you might even write the name MATT in red and MERISSA in green, and then tell a friend that green ink reverses in the mirror, but red ink doesn't. Of course it doesn't have anything to do with the color. All the letters in the boy's name have a plane of symmetry down the center, whereas only the *M, I,* and *A* of the girl's name do.

◉ Questions to Draw and Write About

Make a list of objects that you think are not identical to their mirror images. Such an object is sometimes called *asymmetric.* Asymmetric objects cannot be divided in half so that each half is identical to the other. For example, a ball is symmetric, but your foot is not. Your foot is asymmetric. Draw a picture showing how a ball can be divided in half so that each half is the same. Draw a picture of your foot showing how it cannot be divided in half so that each half is the same. Can you write a short paragraph that explains the difference between something that is symmetrical, such as a ball, and something that is not, such as your foot? Go to a dictionary and look up the words *symmetric* and *asymmetric.* Are these definitions helpful, or are they just confusing?

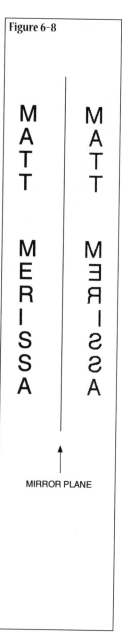

Figure 6-8

MIRROR PLANE

Which of the following objects are asymmetric?

corkscrew

wedding band

clothing iron

ear

flute

telephone wire

candy cane

spoon

Which of the following letters have a vertical plane of symmetry (which can be divided in half from top to bottom so that each half is an exact reflection of the other half)?

O, X, S, R, E, M, B, Z, L, G, I, N, T,

A mirror reverses right and left so that your right hand appears as your left hand when you look in a mirror. Write a short paragraph in which you try to explain why a mirror doesn't reverse top and bottom. You don't have to answer this question. Just write a short paragraph on what you think about it.

Stand in front of a mirror in a darkened room with a flashlight and shine your light on an object appearing in the "mirror room." Holding the light fixed at the mirror, turn around and notice that the object in the real room is lit by the flashlight that shines in the mirror. Write a short paragraph explaining how you think this happens.

Write a short story in which you climb into your bedroom mirror in order to investigate the "mirror-image room" that you see there. Describe what you find in that room. Will the words in books and on your T-shirts look the same? Will the doorknobs be on the same part of the door? Will your shoes and gloves fit properly, or will you have to put your right hand in your left glove and your left shoe on your right foot? Be as imaginative and creative as you can in making up this story.

Have you read the story *Alice in Wonderland* by Lewis Carroll? In parts of this story, the author writes about what it would be like to enter a "looking glass," or "mirror" world.

If you are interested in mirror-image magic, go to the library and check out the book *The Ambidextrous Universe* by Martin Gardner (see Appendix B) and read the short chapter on mirrors and magic.

APPENDIX A

Resources for Effects and Illusions

The magical effects elaborated in Curious Clips, Weird Water, Collapsing Can, Rising and Falling, and Upside Down have all been described many times in a variety of books on magic and science for children.

The magical illusions Incredible Balloon, Amazing String, Unbelievable Quarter, Surprising Spoon and Crazy Cloth have also previously been described in books or other media. However, some of these may be harder to find. References and a few comments about them are provided below.

Incredible Balloon

The materials and directions for Incredible Balloon can be purchased from Hank Lee's Magic Factory (see Appendix C), but the cost will be much greater than if you follow the directions in this book.

This illusion was often performed by Doug Henning on national television. It is also described in the book *Magical Science—Magic Tricks for Young Scientists* by Eric Ladizinsky (see Appendix B).

Amazing String

There are many versions of cut and restored rope and string illusions. The version I've described is outlined in several books, both new and old. An early but well-illustrated description can be found in *Magic and Showmanship: A Handbook for Conjurers* by Henning Nelms (see Appendix B). A variation of this illusion is described in the book *Magic for Beginners* by Harry Baron (see Appendix B).

Unbelievable Quarter

The basic principle involved in the illusion Unbelievable Quarter can be used to pass a variety of objects "through" a film of rubber. Hank Lee's Magic Factory (see Appendix C) sells a variation of this effect that uses a scarf. It's called "Silk in a Balloon," in which a vanished silk scarf magically appears inside a previously inflated, tied-off balloon that has already been shown as empty. I have done the illusion using a small wooden ball. The illusion of passing a coin through a rubber film stretched over a glass is also elegantly described and illustrated in *The Klutz Book of Magic* by John Cassidy and Michael Stroud (see Appendix B). This book is one of the best written and most clearly illustrated books of simple magic available. If you want another book on magic, this is the one to get! The rubber film is provided with the book, but soon wears out. A piece of a large colorless balloon purchased at a party store works just as well.

Surprising Spoon

Basic principles of the illusion Surprising Spoon are described in a NOVA broadcast called "Secrets of the Psychics with James Randi," which aired on National Public Television. More details can be found at James Randi's home page on the World Wide Web.

Crazy Cloth

Crazy Cloth is a variation of an old illusion that has been described in many publications over the years. It has often been used by stage magicians with either paper or cloth. One of the best descriptions (as well as a bit of history of the illusion) can be found in *Mathematics, Magic and Mystery* by Martin Gardner (see Appendix B).

Magic Books

There are thousands of magic books available, and it would be a hopeless task to try to list more than a few of these. However, some are particularly interesting and well written, not too expensive, and appropriate for the classroom. A few of these are listed below. Students and teachers might wish to expand their knowledge of the science and techniques of magic by using the effects and illusions described in these books.

 ## Specifically for Children (Focusing on Magic and Science)

Barr, George. 1987. *Science Tricks and Magic for Young People.* Mineola, New York: Dover Publications. This Dover edition is an unabridged republication of the work first published in 1968 by the McGraw-Hill Book Company under the title *Fun and Tricks for Young Scientists.*

Ladizinsky, Eric. 1994. *Magical Science—Magic Tricks for Young Scientists.* New York: Barnes and Noble Inc. by arrangement with RGA Publishing Group.

For Young Adults and Adults

Baron, Harry. 1991. *Magic for Beginners*. Rocklin, CA: Prima Publishing. This book was originally published by Funk & Wagnalls in 1968.

Baron, Harry. 1995. *Magic for Beginners 2: Card Tricks and Other Close-Up Illusions*. Rocklin, CA: Prima Publishing.

Becker, Herbert. 1994. *All the Secrets of Magic Revealed: The Tricks and Illusions of the World's Greatest Magicians*. Hollywood, FL: Lifetime Books. This book pays homage to a long list of past and present magicians and explains many of the stage illusions you may have seen live or on television. Contains a few simple and straightforward illusions that children can do (including a version of the Incredible Balloon), but many are very complex and expensive. If you want to know how levitation works, how to saw a person in half, how to walk through a brick wall, or how to change your assistant to a tiger, this is the book for you.

Bobo, J. B. 1982. *Modern Coin Magic*. Mineola, NY: Dover Publications.

Burger, Eugene, and Robert Neale. 1995. *Magic and Meaning*. Seattle: Hermetic Press. The authors focus on the psychological meaning of magic, looking at some of the emotional and symbolic aspects. Chapters include "The Magical Experience," "The Shaman's Magic," "Stories of the Origin of Magic," and "Parable Magic." Burger is a full-time professional magician and author, and Neale is a magician and former professor of psychiatry and religion at Union Theological Seminary in New York.

Cassidy, John, and Michael Stroud. 1990. *The Klutz Book of Magic*. Palo Alto, CA: Klutz Press. One of the best-written and well-illustrated books available. And it comes with material and gimmicks!

Doherty, Paul, and John Cassidy. 1994. *The Klutz Book of Magnetic Magic*. Palo Alto, CA: Klutz Press. Another great Klutz book that comes with necessary magnets and gimmicks. This book has well-written and humorous explanations of magnetic phenomena, as well as clear descriptions of the importance of language in creating magical effects.

Edlin, Peter. 1985. *The Magic Handbook*. New York: Alladin Paperbacks. This book was previously published in England under the title *Kingfisher Pocket Book of Magic*. It is a comprehensive guide for young people and contains some history of magic, a general description of props and equipment, and very well illustrated directions for carrying out a variety of illusions. There is also a section on how to perform magic shows, as well as a list of historical references, magical societies, and a list of magic books and magic dealers.

Fulves, Karl. 1988. *Self-Working Handkerchief Magic*. Mineola, NY: Dover Publications.

Gardner, Martin. 1956. *Mathematics, Magic and Mystery*. Mineola, NY: Dover Publications. A unique book that focuses on effects arising from mathematical principles. If you are interested in numbers, mathematics, and magic, this is the book to get.

Gardner, Martin. 1979. *The Ambidextrous Universe*. New York: Charles Schribner's Sons.

Gibson, Walter B. 1995. *Mastering Magic: 100 Secrets of the Great Magicians*. Hollywood, FL: Lifetime Books.

Nelms, Henning. 1969. *Magic and Showmanship: A Handbook for Conjurers*. Toronto: General Publishing Company Ltd.

Tar, Bill. 1976. *Now You See It, How You Don't! Lessons in Sleight of Hand*. Illustrated by Barry Ross. New York: Vintage Books. A very well illustrated, large-size book showing detailed step-by-step instruction for sleight-of-hand illusions using cards, coins, balls, and other common items.

Magic Shops

While this book has focused on effects and illusions that can be done using simple materials from home or items from a grocery or hardware store, thousands more can be done using specially constructed apparatus or materials. These are available from commercial magic shops. The following list was compiled from the World Wide Web and the listing provided by Walter Gibson in his book *Mastering Magic* (see Appendix B). It is not a complete listing and contains only shops that list complete zip codes and telephone numbers. An attempt was made to include primarily those shops that specialize in magic apparatus, effects, and illusions, rather than in costumes, jokes, and novelties.

Absolutely Magic
12 Church St.
Bradford, NH 03221
Tel 603 938 5158

Al's Magic Shop
1012 Vermont Ave. NW
Washington, DC 20005-4901
Tel 202 789 2800

Amazing Beckman
1501 Pike Pl.
Seattle, WA 98101
Tel 206 624 3271

Ben'z Magic Shop
4552 Kirkwood Dr.
Sterling Heights, MI 48310
Tel 313 526 2442

Bishop's Magic Shop
3242 Harlmen Ave.
Riverside, IL 60546-2069
Tel 708 442 9166

BJ's Magic
118–20 14th Rd.
College Point, NY 11356
Tel 718 353 5648

Chattanooga Magic and Fun
4738G Hwy 58
Chattanooga, TN 37416
Tel 423 892 5682; Fax 423 892 1502

Daytona Magic
136 S. Beach St.
Daytona Beach, FL 32114-4402
Tel 902 252 6767

Delben Magic, Inc.
P.O. Box 1835
Spring, TX 77383
Tel 713 353 6618

Don's Magic and Fun Shop
1901 Estero Blvd. No. 8
Ft. Meyers Beach, FL 33931
Tel 813 463 7005

Elmwood Magic & Novelty
507 Elmwood Ave.
Buffalo, NY 14222
Tel 716 886 5653

Fantastic Magic Company
P.O. Box 33156
Granada Hills, CA 91394-3156
Tel 805 252 1142

Fedko Magic Company
13111 Flint Dr.
Santa Ana, CA 92705-1859
Tel 714 538 6044

Geno Munari's Magic
MGM Grand Hotel
3799 Las Vegas Blvd.
S. Las Vegas, NV 89109
Tel 702 798 4789; Fax 702 798 0045

Golden's Magic Wand
P.O. Box 1509
San Marcos, CA 92079-1509
Tel 619 471 0100

Guaranteed Magic
27 Bright Rd.
Hatboro, PA 19040-2023
Tel 215 672 3344

Hank Lee's Magic Factory
P.O. Box 789
Medford, MA 02155
Tel 617 482 8749; Fax 617 395 2034
email: magicFact@aol.com

Hollywood Magic, Inc.
6614 Hollywood Blvd.
Hollywood, CA 90028
Tel 213 464 5610

House of Magic
2025 Chestnut St.
San Francisco, CA 94123-2701
Tel 415 346 2218

Hughes Magic
352 N. Prospect St.
Ravenna, OH 44266
Tel 216 296 4023

Kartay's House of Magic
14-A Braddock Square
Lovely, MD 21502
Tel 301 729 3971

Kogel's Magic
6751 Colbert St.
New Orleans, LA 70124-2240
Tel 504 482 5153

Louis Tannin Inc.
24 West 25th St., 2nd Floor
New York, NY 10010
Tel 212 929 4599; Fax 212 929 4565
email: spinamagic@aol.com

The Magic Connection
6663 Huntley Rd., Ste. F
Columbus, OH 43229
Tel 414 848 8749

Magic House of Babcock
3755 Eels Rd.
Cashmere, WA 98815-9745
Tel 509 782 2730

Magic Industries, Inc.
3309 Broad Rock Blvd.
Richmond, VA 23224
Tel 804 230 1500

Magic Shop of Reno
1 North Virginia
Reno, NV 89501
Tel 702 786 6544

Magic World
327 Clay St.
Moulton, NJ 08850-1445
Tel 201 545 9624

Magical Mysteries
4700 N. 31 Ct.
Hollywood, FL 33021
Tel 305 987 1039

Magical Productions International
1020 N 4th St.
Birthoud, CO 80513-1121
Tel 303 532 0350

Market Magic Shop
1501 Pike Pl., No. 427
Seattle, WA 98101-1542
Tel 206 624 4271

Merlin's Mystical Emporium
363 South Mills, No. 1650
Ventura, CA 93003
Tel 805 639 0044

Mostly Magic Shop
311 D St.
Santa Rosa, CA 95404
Tel 707 523 2842

Mr. E's Magic & Novelties
314-A E. Pershing St.
Springfield, MO 65806
Tel 417 862 1968

Oasis Magic
5723 N. Sultana Ave.
Temple City, CA 91780-2334
Tel 818 286 6412

Showplace Novelty and Magic
50 S. Main St., Ste. 92
Salt Lake City, UT 84144-2019
Tel 801 359 3349

Sterling Magic Manufacturing
20998 Huntwood Ave., Ste. 103
Hayward, CA 94544-7033
Tel 510 487 6319

Steven's Magic Emporium
3238 E. Douglas Ave.
Wichita, KS 67208-3396
Tel 316 683 9582

Sud's Magic
24795 Heil Dr.
Moreno Valley, CA 92553-5878

Top Hat Magic
5555 E. 41st St.
Tulsa, OK 74135-6008
Tel 918 663 5550

Up Your Sleeve Discount Magic
P.O. Box 610
Friendswood, TX 77549-0610
Tel 713 996 5232

Village Magic
152 E. Limestone St.
Yellow Springs, OH 45387
Tel 513 767 1089

Winkler's Warehouse of Wonders
24 Doyle Rd.
Oakdale, CT 06370-1052
Tel 203 859 3474

Wizardz
1000 Universal Center Drive
Citywalk 217
Universal City, CA 91608
Tel 818 506 0066

World of Magic
P.O. Box 584
Green River, UT 84525-0584
Tel 800 771 7012

World of Magic and Fun
3115 Shadow Walk Ln.
Tucker, GA 30084
Tel 404 491 8245

Glossary

air: The invisible mixture of gases in the atmosphere, consisting of about seventy-eight percent nitrogen, twenty-one percent oxygen, and one percent argon. Air also contains small amounts of carbon dioxide, variable amounts of water vapor, and very small amounts of other gases.

asymmetric: Having no symmetry. An asymmetric object cannot be superimposed upon its mirror image.

atom: The smallest part of an element that has the characteristics of that element. All the atoms of any one element are chemically identical. An atom is composed of even smaller particles called *protons, neutrons* and *electrons* (see below). The protons and neutrons, which are much heavier than the electrons, are in the center of the atom—the atomic nucleus. The electrons exist outside the nucleus. The proton has a positive charge equal in magnitude to that of the electron. The neutron has no charge. In a neutral atom the number of electrons is the same as the number of protons, so there is no net charge. If electrons are lost from the atom, a positive ion results (see below). If the atom gains electrons, a negative ion results.

buoyancy: The upward force exerted on a less-dense object floating in a more-dense liquid.

carbon dioxide: A relatively heavy, colorless gas that is formed by the combustion of organic substances with oxygen. It is absorbed from the air by plants in photosynthesis and is converted into complex molecules such as cellulose and sugars. It is also one of the end products of animal metabolism. A carbon dioxide molecule results from the chemical combination of one atom of carbon and two atoms of oxygen.

cell: In biology, a cell is the smallest structural unit of an organism (plant or animal) that can function independently. It consists of one or more nuclei, the cytoplasm (intracellular fluid), and various organelles, all surrounded by a semipermeable cell membrane.

cellulose: A polymeric carbohydrate composed of long chains of glucose molecules. It is the main constituent of the cell wall in most plants.

charge: An excess or deficiency of electrons, small negative particles. An excess of electrons produces a *negative* charge whereas a deficiency of electrons produces a *positive* charge. Positive and negative charges can coexist on a single neutral species, like a water molecule. Such species are called *polar*, and contain a positive pole and a negative pole.

chirality: That property of an object that makes it not superimposable upon its mirror image. The right and left hands are examples of chiral objects. The right hand is not superimposable upon its mirror image. Neither is the left hand. The word chiral comes from the the Greek *cheir*, hand.

chromosome: A long linear strand of DNA (see below) coated with protein that occurs in the nucleus of animal and plant cells. DNA carries the genetic information important in transmitting hereditary information.

close-up-magic: Effects and illusions designed to be performed with the magician very close to the audience.

condensation: The process by which a vapor is changed to a liquid. Condensation is one example of a change of state (change from vapor to liquid, liquid to solid, or the reverse of these processes).

deception: The act of causing someone to believe what is not true.

density: The mass per unit volume of a substance. It is usually specified at a particular temperature and pressure.

DNA: An acronym for **D**oxyribo **N**ucleic **A**cid, a giant polymer molecule that consists of two longs chains of smaller nucleotide molecules. The long chains are twisted into a double helix. The sequence of nucleotide molecules in these chains determines hereditary characteristics.

double helix: The coiled structure of double-stranded DNA (see above) in which the individual strands are linked together to form a spiral configuration.

ductility: That property of a substance (usually a metal) that allows it to be drawn into wire or hammered thin. Ductile substances are easily molded or shaped.

elasticity: That property of a substance that allows it to resume its original shape or form after being stretched, expanded, or deformed.

elastomer: A material, usually a polymer (see below), that is elastic. Rubber is an elastomer.

electricity: The phenomena resulting from the the attraction of particles with opposite charges (positive and negative) and the repulsion of particles with the same charge (i.e., both positive or both negative). Electrical current results when small negative particles (electrons—see below) flow through a wire. When positive and negative particles build up on objects which are then attracted to each other, a spark may jump across the gap between them. *Static electricity* refers to the production of nonmoving charges on objects.

electron: A small, fundamental, negatively charged , subatomic particle. The electron exists outside the nucleus in an atom. It has a very small mass compared to the proton or neutron (see below).

energy: The scientific term refers to the capacity of a physical system to do work. More generally it refers to usable heat or power, like that obtained from a fuel such as oil, gas, or coal.

experiment: An operation or procedure carried out under controlled conditions to test or help establish whether a hypothesis (see below) is true or false.

field: The scientific term relates to a region of space that is characterized by a physical property, such as an electric force caused by opposite charges attracting one another, a magnetic force caused by opposite poles of a magnet attracting one another, or a gravitational force caused by two masses attracting one. another. The force (i.e., electric field, magnetic field or gravitational field) has a specific value at every point in the region of space.

force: The scientific term relating to a quantity that produces an acceleration or movement in the direction of its application. For example, an electrical field produces a force upon a charged object, causing it to move toward an object of opposite charge. More familiar to most of us is a gravitational field (i.e., between the earth and any other object near it) that results in a force on a small object causing it to move toward the larger (i.e., a ball to fall toward the earth).

formula: In chemistry the term refers to a combination of element symbols written together with appropriate subscripts, representing a compound. Subscripts are numbers written below and to the right of an element symbol in a formula to indicate the number of atoms of that element present in the formula. For example, the small 2 between the H and O in the formula for water, H_2O, indicates that a water molecule contains two hydrogen atoms for each oxygen atom.

gas: That state of a substance in which the molecules are very far apart from each other and travel relatively long distances before colliding with other molecules. A gas has no definite shape, but fills the container that holds it. Unlike liquids and solids, gases are easily compressed and will occupy smaller volumes at higher pressures. Another term for gas is vapor.

gene: A hereditary unit that occupies a specific location on a chromosome (see above) and determines a particular characteristic in an organism.

gimmick: A secret piece of equipment used in the creation of an illusion.

glucose: A sugar found in honey, fruits, and blood. It is composed of the elements carbon, hydrogen, and oxygen in the ratios indicated by the subscripts in its formula, $C_6H_{12}O_6$. A common name for glucose is *dextrose.*

gram: A metric unit of mass equal to 1/1000 of a kilogram. A cubic centimeter of water at its maximum density has a mass of about 1 gram. One ounce is about 28.3 grams.

gravity: The force of attraction between any two bodies. This force is directly proportional to the product of their masses (i.e., it increases as they become more massive), but inversely proportional to the square of the distance between them (i.e., it decreases as they become farther apart). See *field,* above.

heat: That form of energy associated with molecular or atomic motion. It is the energy transferred between objects that are at different temperatures. When flowing into a substance this energy causes the temperature to increase. In addition to causing a temperature increase, inward heat flow can cause a solid to melt, a liquid to vaporize, a gas to expand, and substances to undergo chemical changes. When flowing out of a substance, the heat loss causes the temperature of that substance to decrease. Under these conditions, in addition to decreasing in temperature, outward heat flow can cause a gas to decrease in volume and eventually condense, and a liquid to freeze.

hypothesis: An unverified explanation of an observation that needs confirmation by further observations and/or experiments. A tentative explanation.

illusion: A mistaken or erroneous perception or belief. In magic it usually refers to a trick, often involving the vanishing or production of an object. In this book illusions are defined as those magical phenomena that depend upon misdirection (see below), hidden objects, and deception (using both language and physical materials).

ion: A single atom or a group of atoms that has acquired a negative charge by gaining electrons or a positive charge by losing electrons. An atom of sodium, Na, that has lost an electron results in a positive sodium ion, Na^+. An atom of chlorine, Cl, that has acquired an electron, results in the negative chloride ion Cl^-. Positive ions are called *cations*. Negative ions are called *anions*. Table salt, which is sodium chloride, formed from a sodium ion and chloride ion, is an ionic compound with the formula Na^+Cl^- or NaCl.

jute: The fiber obtained from the jute plant *(Corchorus capsularis)*, which commonly grows in Asia. The fiber is commonly used for sacking, cordage, and twine.

law: In scientific terminology a law is a hypothesis that has been proven over and over again so that it is, for all practical purposes, true.

levitation: The illusion of something rising into the air and floating without visible means of support, in apparent defiance of gravity.

liquid: That state of a substance in which the molecules are relatively close to each other, but are not held in rigid positions. They are free to move about throughout the liquid. While a liquid does have a definite volume, it has no definite shape, but instead takes the shape of the container that holds it. Only the top of the liquid, where it does not touch the container, is flat. In lay terms, a liquid is that state of matter in which a substance exhibits an ability to flow.

magic: Using sleight of hand, deception, misdirection, misleading language, creative lying, gimmicks, and materials to create effects and illusions for entertainment. In some cultures magic is that art (using charms, spells, or rituals) purporting to control natural events, effects, or forces by invoking the supernatural.

magician: A person who practices magic.

malleable: Capable of being shaped or formed by hammering or pressure. Metals such as copper, silver, and gold are malleable, and can be made to assume various shapes by hammering and applying pressure to them.

matter: A physical substance that occupies space, has mass, and exists as a solid, liquid, or gas.

metals: Elements that are lustrous, good conductors of heat and electricity, and which are ductile and malleable (see above). Metals are listed on the left and in the middle of the periodic table of the elements. They readily react with nonmetals, losing electrons to form positive ions, while the nonmetals gain electrons to form negative ions. These positive and negative ions are the constituents of the ionic compounds formed when metals react with nonmetals.

micrometer: A device used for measuring very small distances or objects.

misdirection: In magic, the art of drawing the observer's attention away from a secret move. It is one of the most important aspects of magic, and takes much experience and practice.

misperception: A misinterpretation of sensory stimuli that creates false knowledge. In magic, it is often a key element in the creation of an illusion.

molecule: A chemically combined group of two or more like or unlike atoms. A water molecule contains two hydrogen atoms chemically combined with one oxygen atom. A molecule can be represented by a formula. For example, a water molecule is represented by the formula H_2O. A nitrogen molecule contains two nitrogen atoms chemically combined with one another and is represented by the formula N_2.

neutron: A small, fundamental, neutral, subatomic particle that exists, along with protons, in the nucleus of an atom. It is very massive compared to the mass of an electron, but very nearly equal in mass to the proton.

nitrogen: A nonmetallic, neutral, chemically unreactive, gaseous element that composes four-fifths of the air by volume. It occurs as a colorless, odorless, molecule containing two nitrogen atoms (N_2).

observation: The act of seeing, noting, and recording a phenomenon, often involving measuring or other instruments.

oxygen: A nonmetallic, neutral, chemically reactive, gaseous element that composes one-fifth of the air by volume. It occurs as a colorless, odorless, molecule containing two oxygen atoms (O_2). Oxygen readily combines with most other elements and is the gas absorbed by animals when they breathe. It is essential to all life processes. It is also the gas that combines with substances when they undergo combustion. Reactions involving oxygen are often called oxidations.

patter: In magic, it is the storyline, joke, or other type of talk used by a magician in the presentation of an effect or illusion.

pedagogy: The techniques and methods used in the profession of teaching.

perception: An interpretation of sensory stimuli that creates knowledge.

phenomena: An occurrence or fact that is perceived by the senses. It appears real to the mind, regardless of whether its underlying existence is proved or its nature is understood.

polymer: Any one of a number of natural or synthetic large molecules made up of thousands to millions of smaller molecules linked together.

pressure: A force applied uniformly over a surface (often caused by one object or substance on another that is touching it).

props: In magic, this is shorthand for *properties,* the apparatus and other materials used by a magician.

protein: Any one of a large group of complex organic, giant, molecules (polymers) containing mainly the elements of carbon, hydrogen, nitrogen, oxygen, and sulfur. Proteins are composed of long chains of smaller amino acid molecules, linked together. Proteins are fundamental components of all living material. Examples include enzymes, hormones, antibodies, and cell structural material. The protein material in hair is in the form of long helical strands.

proton: A small, fundamental, positively charged, subatomic particle that exists, along with neutrons, in the nucleus of an atom. It is very massive compared to the mass of an electron, but equal in mass to the neutron.

routine: In magic, the order of events that make up an effect or illusion, or a series of effects and illusions that follow one another in a presentation.

rubber: A natural or synthetic, elastic (see above) material used in the formation of many kinds of products such as rubber bands, balloons, tires, and electrical insulation.

science: A method or discipline of observing, identifying, describing, and investigating phenomena in order to provide an explanation for and knowledge about them.

sleight: A skillful movement of the fingers or hands by which a magical effect or illusion is accomplished. It often takes much practice.

sleight-of-hand: The performance of sleights in a presentation of magic.

solid: That state of a substance in which the molecules or ions are packed very closely to each other in regular rigid arrays. The molecules or ions do not move freely about in the solid, but remain fixed in place. A solid has a specific volume and shape and is not compressible.

surface tension: An attractive force experienced by surface molecules in a liquid from the molecules underneath the surface. This attracts surface molecules down into the central mass, causing the surface layer to form a "skin" over the main body of the liquid.

symbol: Something that represents something else by association or resemblance. It can be a material object used to represent something invisible. In chemistry, an element symbol is a single capital letter, or a set of two letters with the first capitalized, which represents one atom of an element or a large collection of atoms of an element. The letters are often derived from English, Latin, or Greek names for elemental substances.

symmetry: Referring to identical form or configuration on opposite sides of a dividing line or a plane, or about a center or an axis.

topography: A graphical representation of surface features of a region on a map, indicating their relative positions and elevations by lines and/or colors.

twine: A string or cord made of two or more threads twisted together. Twine is often made from fibers of jute (see above).

vinegar: A five-percent solution of acetic acid in water, usually containing other materials resulting from its production by fermentation. It is used as a condiment and preservative.

volume: The amount of space taken up by a three-dimensional object or region of space, often expressed in cubic units (i.e., cubic feet or cubic centimeters).

water: A clear liquid compound (at room temperature) containing the elements hydrogen and oxygen. The formula for water is H_2O.

Index

Author photo by Sally McCay, The University of Vermont